ELNA:

A Danish Blossom
in
Urban Blight

Elna:

A Danish Blossom
in
Urban Blight

by
Harold E. Olsen

Editor: John W. Nielsen

Lur Publications
Danish Immigrant Archive

Dana College

Published by Lur Publications, Dana College, Blair, Nebraska, 68008.

First edition.

ISBN 0-930697-15-4

Logo designed by Elizabeth Solevad Nielsen
Designed by Thomas S. Nielsen, 2066 Colfax St., Blair, NE 68008
Printed by MicroSmart Printing & Graphics, 1740 Washington St., Blair, NE 68008

Printed in the United States of America

Contents

Illustrations

Editor's Introduction

I, perhaps like many others, first encountered Elna Olsen in the series of short articles that her son, Harold, wrote for **Church and Life**. Now in this book he has collected those articles into a single volume which follows Elna from her girlhood in Denmark, through her arrival in America, her romance and marriage, the birth of her two children and her abandonment by her husband, ending with her determined resolution to overcome adversity and succeed as an individual and mother. Many undoubtedly will feel that it is unfortunate that the book ends with Harold's ordination, but that event certainly marked the end of one phase of her life. The reader cannot help but note the pride of her son as he traces Elna's challenges and triumphs up to this event which was so important to both of them.

Because the chapters of this book had formed a series of vignettes that appeared in **Church and Life** over a period of several years, many explanatory references had to be included to refresh the reader's memory as to the identity of some person or organization or the location of some institution or factory. Now, because they are appearing in close sequence, most of these references have been deleted. What was necessary in one format is redundant in another.

In submitting the text of this book for publication, Harold Olsen acknowledged that his motive was not only to honor his mother, although that was primary, but also to remind the Danish-American community of the Midwest that there was a similar and equally important concentration of Danes in the East. What is more, this book shifts from a rural to an urban setting, opening up another oft-neglected aspect of Danish immigration.

Danish words and phrases have been set in italics except where they are a part of the intermingled language of the immigrants when English had not yet been mastered and Danish was being lost or deliberately avoided. An index of most persons and places mentioned in the book is provided. Because Elna is the subject of the book and appears on almost every page, she is not referenced in the index.

Harold Olsen not only has written the text but has provided the pictures that enhance the book. Thomas S. Nielsen has created the layout and design, and Birgit Flemming Larsen has offered invaluable assistance with the Danish references as well as proof-reading the entire manuscript. Ted Latwaitis has produced the cover and other computer designs. To each of these individuals who has eased my task, I express my thanks.

John W. Nielsen
Dana College
February 12, 2004

x

About the Author

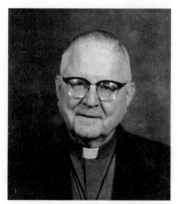

Harold E. Olsen

Harold E. Olsen is a retired pastor of the Evangelical Lutheran Church in America. Ordained in 1950 by one of the predecessor church bodies of the ELCA, Pastor Olsen served congregations of the Danish Evangelical Lutheran church in America in Wisconsin, Oregon, and Iowa before being elected secretary of the Iowa Synod of the Lutheran Church in America upon the formation of that church body in 1962. As a Pastor of the LCA he served two administrative posts and a congregation in the state of Kansas.

Pastor Olsen has traveled extensively throughout the world in the interest of missions - having visited mission fields in India, Burma, Liberia, Ghana, Tanzania and Mexico. Travels of personal interest through the years took him to Norway, Sweden and Denmark.

Early in his career Pastor Olsen was recognized for his leadership in the Lutheran Church in the United States. In 1969 he was recognized by Grand View College in Des Moines for distinguished service to the college. Six years later, he was recognized by the Lutheran School of Theology in Chicago "for his personal counsel to the pastors of the Iowa Synod as well as his counsel in the field of stewardship. His work with congregations affected by shifts in population was noted." Later in his career he was honored in being chosen to represent the LCA in the Lutheran Council of the U.S.A.

Following his retirement in 1983 Pastor Olsen spent several years in the business community - moving in 1989 to northwest Arkansas where he still serves actively his church and community.

December 12, 2003

xi

Elna in Danish Dress

From Denmark
to
the United States
of
America

Carl and Jensine Jespersen
with the six older children.
Elna, the eldest, stands
directly in front of her father.

The Laumark farm where Elna was born

Life Prepares a Young Lady for a Trip to America

"Elegance!" A modest term in describing Elna Jespersen Laumark's life at age 21. Only months before she had been a student at Roskilde Folkehøjskole. Now she was sharing in some of Copenhagen's richest social life.

Her role was labeled "housekeeper," but her privileges, if not her duties, were to share in the rich social life of Copenhagen's most eligible bachelor, who at that moment in time was a member of the Danish Legislature (*Folketinget*). Elna shared vicariously in much of this man's life, but on a variety of occasions occupied the chair of an unavailable companion.

The Royal Theater, museums, acrobatics at Tivoli, lectures at the university were among the many treats. And more exciting still, was when she was simply given the tickets to take her best friend to some cultural event in one of Europe's leading cities.

It seemed too good to be true. Life had not always been that way for Elna. On the contrary, it had been a very difficult life for her in her earlier years.

Her father, a soldier in the Danish Army with the rank of captain, was assigned a tour of duty in Denmark's capital city. There he met Jensine, Elna's mother, with a less than responsible courtship to follow. Elna was born "prematurely" as the first of nine children in a marriage that took place in the Hanbjerg Church in northern Jutland. Shortly after the marriage Carl Jespersen and his pregnant bride took up residency at "*Laumark*" - the "low field" - that belonged to Carl's father, who had farmed in the Hanbjerg parish for many years.

As the other eight children came in rapid succession, it became increasingly difficult for Elna's father to make provision for all of them. The excessive use of alcoholic drink used up much of the resources and made a "workaholic" father a "taskmaster" of his children. Elna, being the eldest, experienced much of the hardship of this situation.

On Elna's eighth birthday, it was determined that "she no longer is needed at home" and she was "farmed" out as an assistant to the cook at an estate in a nearby community. The work was hard. Included in her duties were the daily milking of the family cow, the gathering of eggs, the slaughter of chickens and the subsequent plucking and drawing. Even in temperate Denmark the kitchens were hot and humid - less than pleasant to say the least.

Now and then this difficult work was marked by great events, cherished events. While it never was clear to Elna why King Christian X was visiting her host family, it was one of the greatest thrills of a young girl's life to be hoisted high by the King and to be allowed a moment on his lap as he inquired about her. In retrospect she often said it didn't matter why the King came. What did matter is that she experienced the King's love for his people - even those who did the menial tasks in the home.

Roskilde Folkehøjskole did not come for many years, but it did so at the urging of her rural employer, who himself had tasted in the late 19th century some of the richness of the folk school movement. A wealth of Danish heritage flowed into young students as they participated in the offerings of the various folk schools. Jeppe Aakjær, Adam Oehlenschläger, N. F. S. Grundtvig, Thomas Kingo and Hans Brorson were all contributors to the richness that was to infuse the lives of the young students, Elna included.

The folk dances and the gymnastics, that provided for the fun and exercise attendant to a rich life, were a vital part of Denmark's cultural infusion into the souls of young Danes who availed themselves of the riches of the folk school. At age 40, Elna relived the riches that had come to her and she could still stand on her head and walk the length of her kitchen (approximately 20 feet) on her hands. And as has already been noted, it was but a brief vault from Roskilde to "housekeeper" for Denmark's most eligible bachelor and one of Denmark's outstanding legislative leaders.

When you are having fun, it is difficult to be aware of other factors which also shape the lives of people. And those factors often interrupt. They did so for Elna, whose father and mother had one more difficult assignment for her.

The altar and baptismal font of the
Hanbjerg Church where Elna was baptized.

A Letter From Home

The excitement of Denmark's largest city and the exceptional social opportunities which were part of Elna's employment as housekeeper for one of Denmark's leading legislators paled against letters from Laumark (the low field) near the town of Hanbjerg where her father sought to make a living for himself, his wife and his six children who were still at home. The letters did not come often, usually once a month. Postage was very expensive for anything more. The monthly letters brought news of brothers and sisters who grew inspite of the limited resources and the rigors of farm life. Now and then there was a comment about "Rollo," the family dog, who was missed almost as much as were the sibling children.

The letter which came on the first Tuesday in April seemed appropriately timed. Easter was near at hand and maybe this was an Easter greeting. (Christian holidays were an important part of the life of the Jespersen family). But the letter was not an Easter greeting. The letter was different from all of those which had come in previous deliveries. There were no comments about Elna's brothers and sisters. There was no comment about the dog. This letter came with a request, a request that was to change Elna's life dramatically.

Several years before the letter in question, the family had received a visit from Uncle Peter Hansen (Jensine's brother) and his wife *Tante Marie*, who had emigrated to America many years earlier and had done very well in their newfound land. Peter and his wife, though they had fared well, were childless, and on the occasion of their visit they mentioned that they would be glad to help out the Jespersen family by taking one of their children as one of their own. Being even more specific Peter had said, "Should you ever find that you are unable to care for all of your children, we would be glad to take Christine as our daughter." Now, four years later with Christine at 16 years of age, that invitation loomed large for the Jespersen family which was suffering severe financial distress.

The invitation weighed heavily on Carl Jespersen, father of both Elna and Christine, but it tore more painfully at the heart of Jensine, their mother, who wondered if, in fact, she could let Christine go. When the letter to Elna was written, the painful decision had been made. Christine could go, but she could not go alone. The stories of the destinies of unchaperoned young women made it clear that to send a young girl, such as Christine, to a far away land without a responsible adult would be total disaster for all concerned. To be sure, she would be safe in the new land, but the journey could not be seen as safe. Elna was a logical choice to be the one who should go along..

The letter, which arrived on the Tuesday before Easter in 1922, shared the agony of the household at home. It left Elna petrified for what seemed to be several days. "America!" Exciting, yes! But now? In the midst of an existing dream?

When the numbness wore off, Elna gave serious thought to the contents of that "Easter" letter. She was sure that the plan had been carefully thought out at Laumark. The conditions seemed generous enough. She would be given a ticket to America by her father and mother. With work opportunities "abundant" in America, it would only be a short time before she could return to Denmark for another adventure. But it was not the lure of a trip to America, nor was it the terms under which she would travel that caused Elna to give an affirmative answer. It was the love for a younger sister and her dutiful respect for her father and mother who had always been there that caused Elna to accept the assignment placed upon her.

It was with tears in her eyes that she made her decision known to her employer, whose wisdom did little to dissuade her. In a few days there was a trip home (her belongings there were few) to say good-bye, with even larger tears, to her family and with her sister to depart for Copenhagen where they would board a ship called *S.S. Oscar II* for America. America! It had not been on Elna's mind, but now it was before her at every turn.

Even Rollo, the dog was to get a kiss good-bye.

Preparing for the American Journey

The interval between the decision to respond favorably to the request of her parents to chaperone her sister, Christine, to America and the actual departure date evaporated for Elna, as it did for all who were involved in the adventure.

For Elna's parents - and especially her mother, Jensine - it was correspondence with Jensine's brother Peter and his wife, *Tante* Marie. At the very best a letter from Denmark took fifteen days to arrive at an American destination. If such a letter received instant response, it was another fifteen days for a return letter to arrive at its destination in Denmark. During the round trip of the correspondence from Europe life continued on both sides of the Ocean.

In Denmark it was carrying on the activity of the farm - cows to herd and to milk, fields to be cultivated and planted and trips to town (20 km) for business and pleasure. Inside the house there were garments to be made and/or repaired. There were the moments of loving exchange between people who loved each other and who knew that life sometimes took a turn which caused permanent separation even among those most closely united. There were stories of people who had set out for America with a plan to return to Denmark when their fortune had been made who for all kinds of reasons, including the lack of financial resources, did not return to the families they had.

The plan at the Jespersen (Laumark) farm always affirmed and reaffirmed the notion that Elna's trip to America would be a short-lived one. (She was to insure the safety of herself and her sister on the journey to America and with a bit of luck and maybe some help from Uncle Peter she could gather up enough money to return to Denmark in, at most, a year. Certainly, no longer than that. Hopefully a good deal less than that.)

In America life moved at a fairly fast pace for Uncle Peter and *Tante* Marie. Their childless state made it possible for them to attend all kinds of social and community functions. They often attended meetings of the Danish Brotherhood Lodge and on the major holidays made an effort to participate in the Danish Church community. Christmas, Easter and Pentecost were important days for the Hansens, and with some effort both Peter and his wife could be found at the worship services at St. Stephens Danish Evangelical Lutheran Church (*Den Danske Kirke*) in Perth Amboy, New Jersey.

Now, there was a letter from Denmark that spoke to a request that

Uncle Peter had made on a not-so-recent trip to that country. When the letter arrived, Peter and Marie Hansen were not quite as ready to have a "half grown" child in their home as they had thought earlier. It took some days of serious deliberation in their home, before they could respond with enthusiasm to their own suggestion that Christine become as their child.

Summer days are pleasant in Denmark. They are also long because of the latitudinal location of Denmark. By mid summer (*Sankt Hansdag*) the work had subsided some and there was time to reflect on the whole idea of moving part of the family to America. For Elna those moments of reflection included memories, fond memories, of her days at Roskilde Folk High School. The songs of her heritage which she sang there, many of them she had memorized, filled her head, and soon her body responded with the rhythm and steps of Denmark's folk dances. The poetry of Jeppe Aakjær welled up in her soul and tugged at her "Danish" heart. The bright lights of subsequent days in Copenhagen with its cultural and social opportunities gave her pause - if only in fleeting moments - about her decision to escort her sister to an unknown land.

As she mused about the unknown she was filled alternately with excitement and apprehension about what her few months in America would be like. Could she share there some of the great memories of her earlier life, and would there be people there who would understand how precious all of that was to her? Would the Danes be gathered in one place or would they be scattered about a land which was said to be quite a bit larger than Denmark? Would there be a work opportunity that could provide for her livelihood and a return trip ticket to Denmark? Uncle Peter and *Tante* Marie had said they wanted Christine, but would they be as willing to have another Jespersen child, young lady, in their home until she could get settled.

Rollo, the dog, suspected that there was something going on. Life was a bit more tense than usual and activity was at an all-time high. Every now and then, it was Elna's turn to have a little chat with him about her great adventure. As if to understand, Rollo would cock his head in loving affirmation.

And now, the time had come. The buggy had been loaded. Each in his or her turn, hugged the two young women who were off to America. And, oh yes, Rollo, the dog, got his good-bye kiss. Before the tears could dry, Carl Jespersen grasped the reins, and the three of them headed for Holstebro, where Elna and Christine would board a train for their trip to the great unknown.

Two Young Ladies Set Sail

There was a deep sadness among the passengers of the buggy that was headed for Holstebro. Memories of wonderful family experiences flashed in and out of the minds of all three. Carl Jespersen was sure that the right decision had been made when it was decided to send Christine to America. He was also sure that it was the right thing to ask Elna to chaperone her sister on the trip. But quietly within him was the tug that did not want to let the children go.

Elna had memories which were in addition to those of wonderful family moments when she was very young. There was her first job that took her away from home at an early age. There were the days as a student at Roskilde Folk High School. There were her more mature years as a domestic in Copenhagen. All of these memories took turns dancing through a mind that was also filled with notions of further adventure.

For Christine, it was a chance to be away from home, but still to be with family. Home and destiny exchanged places with every "plop" of the horses hooves. She would miss most her younger sister, Julianne, or "Julle" as they called her. She would miss Rollo who often lay his chin in her lap and groan a groan of contentment, before dismissing himself to lay at the hearth of the family home. She already felt many, many kilometers from home - even before the city of Holstebro came into view.

The sadness soon turned to excitement in anticipation of the train ride down the west coast of Jylland, the east bound trip across to the ferries which were to take the trains to the Islands of Fyn and Sjælland to Copenhagen's harbor where *S.S.Oscar II* awaited their boarding. The train was immaculate, and the scenery was beautiful - filled with harvest colors, for the grains were nearly ready for cutting. White caps and sea gulls decorated the beautiful blue of the seas surrounding the Danish islands - providing another kind of beauty. As they moved closer and closer to their point of departure from their beloved Denmark, the excitement turned to apprehension and, in fleeting moments, outright fear of what lay before them.

Getting around in Copenhagen was not a difficult task since Elna had been well exposed to the city in her earlier life. Most of the travelers with whom they were to rub elbows were fellow Danes, but not a few were from other parts of Northern Europe. Important to this part of their journey was that they were to meet *Tante* Minnie who would be

10

LIST O STATES IMMIGRATION OFFIC

ALL ALIENS arriving at a port of continental United States from a foreign ; States, or a port of another insular possession, in whatsoever class they travel, MUST be
STEERAGE PASSENGERS ONLY

S. S. • Oscar II •   Arriving at Port of _____ New York

No. on List.	HEAD-TAX STATUS. (This column for use of Government check only.)	NAME IN FULL		Age.			Calling or occupation.			By whom passage paid?		Whether ever before in the United States; and if so, when and where? If yes—			Whether going to join a relative or friend; what relative or friend, and his and complete address.
		Family name.	Given name.	Yrs. Mos.	Sex			No. on List							
		Jensen	Dagmar Mary	27	f	m wife	1	yes	husband					husband: jens N.V.Jens 1653 Adison Str. Chica
		Findsen	Carl Chr.	21	m	m shopa	1	yes	self					brother: Jørgen Finds Henningsens Court Co. friend, Wade Madsen 3
		Olsen	Helge	22	m	m electr	3	yes	self					Bread str Central F
		Kjær	Gustav S.	21	m	s bookke	4	yes	self					brother: Holger Kjar Produce Exchange, New
		Laumark	Elna J.	22	f	s servan	5	yes	self					uncle: Peder Hansen 21, Thomas Str. South
			Laura K.J.	16	f	s servan	6	yes	self					
		Andersen	Mathilde K.	29	f	m wife	1	no	self					husband: Emil Anderse 2426, Spaulding Ave, C
UNDER 14			Tove L.J.	1	f	s child	8	no	mother					father
		Andersen	Edith O.E.	30	f	s nurse	9	no	self					cousin:

**A page (partial) of the Manifest of the ship, *S.S.Oscar II*
on which Elna and her sister Christine sailed from Denmark.**

sailing on the same ship that the two young ladies were to be on, and
there had been a promise from her that she would "look after them" and
see to it that they got to their destination in America. (Minnie was not
really an aunt except by virtue of being a sister to *Tante* Marie in whose
home Christine was to live.) It turned out to be of little comfort for the
two new travelers. *Tante* Minnie had her own agenda, and it hardly
included watchfulness over two travel novices whom she had never
included in her thoughts as family members. Occasionally there would
be a glance in the direction of the girls, but only enough so that she could
say with some degree of honesty that she had escorted them to America
and their destination in that land.

The time for boarding the ship for America came quickly. The
young ladies found their cabin after some shuffling about on the lower
decks. They had precious little baggage so there was not much to look
after in that regard. As they chatted with some relief about being on
board, they heard the engines of the ship increase their revolutions and
soon the ship was gliding to the position from which it would be full
steam ahead.

October 12, 1922 was a beautiful day and the beginning of many beautiful days at sea. "The Atlantic was as still as a lake," they observed. October 12th followed Elna's birthday by two days which made it necessary for Elna to celebrate only with the excitement and the moments of apprehension which were hers on her departure from Europe.

The ship, which was of Scottish registry, was not very clean in the judgment of the two young ladies. Perhaps it was no worse than any public transportation - not designed for luxury. To the two young and fastidious ladies, the ship was "dirty." They adjusted, but not without strong desire to be gone from that vessel and to be gone soon.

The dirt became exaggerate by the fact that there were not many of their age aboard the ship. It also became clear that among the passengers were a significant number who had known nothing but poverty all of their lives, and standards for those who had grown up in such circumstances were sometimes less than what the two young women had come to expect.

To change the monotony of twelve days at sea, the young ladies would venture to the upper decks where they could look out at the sea. To minister to their souls they often hummed a tune from their childhood, occasionally a hymn by N. F. S. Grundtvig or Hans Brorson. They mused about many things. Would life in America be kind to them? Would they ever return to Denmark? (That was the plan for Elna, but lurking within that plan were fleeting moments of doubt.) Would there be a job? That had been promised as part of the plan. Would there be other young people with whom they could share the adventure?

Their musings were sometimes interrupted by the several young boys who quite naturally spoke the universal language of young people on an adventure. Christine was especially pretty, and the young men did not fail to notice that. Elna had a regal beauty, made more royal by the assignment which was hers. She did not go unnoticed, but the young men sensed her responsibility and knew instinctively that they would not get her full attention. The calmness of the sea was not always matched by calmness within for all the reasons suggested above.

Morning on the twelfth day at sea arrived, with the harbor of New York in full view to those who lined the rails of the ship. Now the attention of all on board was on New York and the new land in which all of the ship's passengers were to make their way.

Tagged for New Jersey

New York was in view, but only to be seen. It was yet to be experienced. But that was soon to change. With engines now at fewer revolutions than they had been for twelve days, the ship that carried Elna and Christine across the Atlantic seemed to be in a glide. Deck hands, who had been fairly casual in their duties while the ship was at "full speed ahead," now were busy getting ready to cast lines to the tug boats that were to take them with precision and safety to the mooring platform at Ellis Island.

Small craft increased in numbers the closer the ship got to the Hudson River. Every now and then there was a smell more pungent and foul than anything they had experienced anywhere along the way. The culprits were the "garbage wagons," barges filled with the city's refuse, headed out to sea to dump their cargo where perishable material would disappear while non-biodegradable materials sank to the bottom or washed ashore on the nearby beaches. Swooping over the dumped garbage were the sea gulls and other scavengers of the sea, diving once and again at those who nibbled on refreshments that the ship's passengers had brought along for their trip.

Smells intensified as the ship lazed its way to the appointed docking area. Raw sewage, mixed with industrial waste pooled where the Hudson met the Atlantic, sending vapors laden with the gases of the percolating debris of millions of people who had collected in the port cities of the New York metropolitan area. The environment hardly offered much of a welcome.

Through the unpleasantness and haze that formed from the emission of smoke and gases from the industrial side of the harbor, the Statue of Liberty came into view. Miss Liberty was an imposing lady, but gave no evidence of American hospitality except that she was part of the distant harbor for which the refugees from Europe had looked.

Even if the girls had been close enough to read the inscription at the base of the statue, they would not have been able to read the words of welcome which included words well-known to those who have read their American history:

> Give me your tired, your poor,
> Your huddled masses yearning to breathe free,
> The wretched refuse of your teaming shore;
> Send these, the homeless, tempest tossed to me,
> I lift my lamp beside the golden door.

It seemed like "forever" for the ship to be secured, for the engines to slow down to a "purr," for the gangplanks to be put in place and for disembarking to occur. It seemed like an "eternity" with lots of time to think and to reflect on life and its destinies. In Elna's mind was a powerful message which arose out of the cultural and spiritual revival of the nineteenth century in Denmark. That revival had filled her with an indelible impression of who she was, regardless of the worldly circumstance.

> "I am a Laumark, a child of Carl and Jensine Jespersen, and a child of God, baptized at Hanbjerg in the parish church there, steeped in the Danish culture and the Christian faith - not alone but with my history and my faith and with a song in my heart."

The thoughts probably did not come packaged quite that neatly, but they flashed quickly through her head and reminded her of who she was. And how important it was that Elna could think these thoughts for soon she would not be the person that she knew herself to be, but part of "the huddled masses," herded with all of the others who entered New York harbor that day to be "processed" for further delivery. For Elna and Christine that processing began with the prodding and pushing of a vast number of people to a station where they were to be shunted on to the "Scandinavian" desk for the necessary paperwork and medical examinations. At no time, and nowhere before, had they been treated with less dignity.

As soon as they were through with their paperwork and their medical examination (no privacy in this process) and had bathed their exposed extremities and any body abrasions in potassium chloride, they were "Tagged for New Jersey." In bold and dark black letters the tag said, "**HOBOKEN.**"

The Danish Lutheran Church Ministers

Still being herded, Elna and Christine were literally shoved on to a harbor ferry that took people from Ellis Island to rail terminals where each immigrant was to find his or her way. The bold tag marked HOBOKEN made it clear where the immigration authorities were to direct Elna and Christine. Once the ferry was loaded, it took only minutes to reach Hoboken where again the two young ladies were herded to a large chamber in the railroad station, called the "waiting room." There appeared to be more freedom of movement at the Hoboken railroad station. American "natives" - those who had arrived earlier - scurried with determination to their gates. Most were oblivious to the new arrivals. The girls felt a bit more free than they had felt since disembarking at Ellis Island, captive only by their own emotions

Elna and Christine waited at the railroad station for what had become a routine time of waiting. They were waiting for a young man whose name was Hans Rasmussen. They had no description, but he would be able to make his identity known by what he knew about them. Elna and her sister knew nothing of the Danish community nor of any of its activity. They knew that they had some family in New Jersey that they hardly knew, and they knew that there was an address to which they were going which was 17 Thomas Street, South River, New Jersey, but beyond that they knew nothing.

What they did not know was that like all other ethnic groups, the Danes had found a location for themselves and to undergird themselves upon their arrival on a distant shore, they had formed several significant groups - chief among them "The Danish Church" (St. Stephen's Danish Evangelical Lutheran Church on Broad Street in Perth Amboy), The Danish Brotherhood and Sisterhood Lodges, the Dania Society, and the Danish Young Peoples Society. While none of these groups had formal programs for meeting their late arriving "cousins," they all had members who were sensitive to the problems encountered by new arrivals and offered their services in meeting ships and trains for people tagged for New Jersey.

Hans Rasmussen, who was active in the Young Peoples Society and who also attended regularly the worship services at the "Broad Street Church," was one of those who felt it important to be of service to new arrivals from Denmark. It was at the Broad Street Church that an aunt and uncle of Elna and Christine had come to know Hans and his dedication to serve, so months before the young girls were to arrive he had been engaged to be the one to meet the young ladies at Hoboken.

15

There was a good deal of apprehension as the young ladies in the train station at Hoboken waited for the young man for whom they only had a name. The apprehension was not only related to the fact that he would be a stranger, but more importantly that there were those at the points of entry into the country that were not motivated by honorable intentions. The term "white slavery" probably did not exist in Denmark as a term, but the girls had been cautioned against offers that sounded too good to be true.

Hans circled the ladies a number of times - eavesdropping on their conversation - hoping to pick up enough information so that he could approach them with respect and integrity. That moment came fairly soon, and Hans proceeded to set forth his credentials, clearly enough so that they agreed to go with him.

The train ride to Perth Amboy seemed like a long ride, even though it was only about 23 miles. The train stopped many times with an accompanying call for the upcoming station. People left and entered the train without fanfare, and the train moved on, screeching its way to the next place and finally, Perth Amboy.

It was a short bus ride from the station at Perth Amboy to 17 Thomas Street in South River where the welcome was more apprehensive than welcoming to the two young ladies who still wondered if a right decision had been made in Denmark.

In a few days they would attend St. Stephen's Danish Evangelical Lutheran Church, where Elna was to meet Peter Hansen's sister, Karen and her husband Rudolf, with whom she was to stay until she could find employment and begin her plans for her return trip to Denmark. With the first Sunday behind them, it would now be days and sometimes weeks before the sisters who had become very dependent upon one another would have opportunity to share their experiences.

Language,
Laughter
and
Love

A Lady, Her Language and Laughter

Karen and Rudolf Hansen had come to America in the late 90s of the nineteenth century. Life had been good to them in America. With excellent carpenter skills, Rudolf set out quite early in his years in America to create a business of his own. Never a large contractor, Rudolf had done well in the home building business, and by the time Elna and Christine arrived in America in 1922, Rudolf was already retired to a respectable residence on New Brunswick Ave in South River, New Jersey. In addition to being well appointed the Hansen home stood at the front end of a building lot that had a backyard large enough to accommodate a large vegetable and flower garden from which they gathered a good deal of their retirement living.

Elna was to live with Karen and Rudolf, but the arrangement was to be temporary - "until Elna could find employment" preferably with "live-in" accommodations. (There was no question about the kind of work that she would do. Clearly, it should be in the kitchen in one of the homes of a successful family who could afford domestic help.) It did not take long for Elna to be placed. Having been in business, Rudolf knew a number of entrepreneurs and through them the word was passed that Elna was available for work.

In just a few days Elna reported for work at the home of Edwin Prentiss, a man who had been very successful in the lumber business and from whom Rudolf Hansen purchased materials regularly. Rudolf had talked to Edwin Prentiss personally on one of his trips to the lumberyard for materials to sub-divide his garden, and as a result of that conversation the usual period of waiting and apprehension became very short.

Edwin Prentiss was a gentle man and good to his employees, both at his place of business and at home. Elna, who was treated with utmost respect, was to be the assistant to Helga Petersson, who had been with the Prentiss family for many years. From Helga she not only was to learn the routine of the Prentiss home, but also enough English so that she could function on those occasions when Helga was absent - by prior agreement or by virtue of seniority. The plan was that Elna was to have Sundays after breakfast off together with Thursdays after the noon-time duties were complete, usually about two in the afternoon. She was to assist at all other occasions - among them a number of elegant parties for the elite of the community.

18

The arrangement was splendid because it offered an opportunity for Elna to attend the worship service at "the Broad Street Church" in Perth Amboy, if, and when, transportation became available. It also gave opportunity to attend the meetings of the Danish Young Peoples' Society which met in a rented hall in Perth Amboy on Thursday evenings. Both filled Elna's life with the same spirit that had filled her life in the country of her birth, childhood and youth.

At the worship services the singing was robust with hymns of favorite authors such as N.F.S. Grundtvig, Thomas Kingo, Hans Brorson and others of the period of Danish renewal in the mid-nineteenth century. The sermons varied in quality, but they often spoke to a lonesome soul in a foreign land.

At "the Hall," as it became known, there were the folk songs of Denmark, together with its national songs and hymns, some very old and others of a later time. "Hild dig vor Fane" and "Der er et Yndigt Land" were favorites. "Kong Christian stod ved højen mast" was not far behind. They had left Denmark physically, but in spirit they were ever there in prayer and song.

All seemed to go very well for Elna. Her charm - yes, her charisma - took her through some moments which otherwise could have brought her spirit low. Language often became a stumbling block, but also the occasion for much laughter.

One occasion for laughter came almost immediately after her employment when Helga sent Elna to the breakfast table of Edwin Prentiss. With coffeepot in hand, Elna curtsied before offering to fill Mr. Prentiss' cup. During the brief exchange, Mr. Prentiss noted that between the two cooks they had failed to put the mustard on the table - a condiment that always topped his "sunny side up" eggs. After the ceremonial bowing and pouring had taken place, Mr. Prentiss asked Elna in as brief a manner as he could muster: "Would you please get me some mustard?" "Oh, yes," said Elna, listening attentively to words that she thought were to follow. Mr. Prentiss repeated his request, but was sure that Elna had not understood the second time, either. With some exasperation in his voice he continued with a request that Helga be summoned. The mustard was delivered almost instantly.

The difficulty had been that the word "mustard" sounded in the ears of the recent immigrant like the Danish word, "Moster," - the term for "mother's sister" or "aunt." How could this newly arrived little lady know that Mr. Prentiss was asking for sennep, the Danish word for Mr. Prentiss' request? How could she know many of those strange English words that enveloped her at almost every turn.

19

Would that the whole world spoke Danish, but, alas, it did not! Fortunately for Elna, this new world was kind and understanding and patient. *"Ja! Gud! Du ska' ha' tak!"* was often her prayer. (Yes, God, You deserve thanks.) In addition there was a word of thanks from the gentle man, whose close friends called him Edwin.

A Young Lady's Soul and Her Social Life

Life at the Edwin Prentiss home was not all work. (Even that which was work didn't seem like work. Elna enjoyed the kitchen and Helga, who presided over the fare there.) When the dishes were done and a bit of planning for the next meal had been completed, Elna was free to enjoy her private quarters in the home.

There, in what was a modestly appointed bedroom-sitting room, Elna often just sat, running through her mind the early years of her life, wondering on many occasions how it was going back at Laumark, the farmstead where she had spent her early years and where her family still lived. Through her mind would go the hymns and songs of Denmark - sometimes so vividly that the thoughts took on sound and she found herself singing the hymns and songs with a passion. The singing took her home where those hymns and songs had been learned. She thought about Viggo, Dagmar, Karna, Martin, Peter, Christian and Julle - brothers and sister that she had left behind. She mused about Rollo - the family dog and wondered how they all were doing.

Her musings often moved her to write letters inquiring about "*dem alle*" (all of them). Along with her questions were observations of her new surroundings. She described the Prentiss family and the spacious home which was theirs. She shared a bit about South River and its neighboring town of Sayreville. Neither of them were farm communities - mostly manufacturing and the processing of products which had a world market. She soon discovered and shared the fact that not all of the people of the area were English speaking, nor were they caught up with a common ethic. To make ones way through town was like touring Europe in miniature. Neighborhoods throughout the area were ethnic conclaves where immigrants found families and foods and festivals which they had known in Europe.

Occasionally, Elna addressed the original plan for her "short trip to America to 'deliver' her sister, Christine, to the home of Peter Hansen" and a return trip to Denmark when she saved enough money to purchase a ticket. (The return ticket had not been in the package. Had there been enough money for that, there would have been no need to send Christine to America.) As time went on, the idea of a return trip to Denmark seemed to become more and more remote. As a consequence, not all thoughts entertained by Elna addressed her past. With each passing week the focus turned more and more to life in America.

While there was a significant number of Danes in the part of New Jersey that belonged to the New York metropolitan area, they were not concentrated as some of the other groups were whose numbers were much larger. Perth Amboy seemed to be a center where the Danes were most distinguishable as a group, and Elna went there as often as her free time would permit - contingent, of course, on the graciousness of those who could supply transportation for the journey of only a few miles.

Sunday morning was very important to Elna, and she attended church at "the Broad Street Church" whenever that was possible, but Thursday evenings offered opportunity to socialize with her fellow Danes. There was always something "down at the hall" (the gathering place in Perth Amboy) - usually planned by the Danish Young Peoples' Society. Folk dancing and gymnastics were high on the list, and holiday parties, centering on the dates of significance to their heritage, often took on more significance than they had in Denmark.

Fastelavn (the Danish equivalent of *Mardi Gras*) was a major celebration. The fifth of June, *Grundlovsdag* (Constitution Day), often gave rise to a kind of patriotism rarely seen in Denmark. Pre-Christmas parties called for creative crafts which would adorn a tree hauled in from the streets by strong young men. Æbleskiver, *frikadeller*, *skinke*, *sild* and coffee were favorite foods. A schottische, a waltz, a polka were among the favorite dances providing a good time for all. The exhilaration of those evenings sustained their souls as they entered into yet another week of work.

Holidays and heritage were not the only thing of interest at the gathering at "the Hall." For the young women, it was often the attraction of young and vigorous men from their homeland. And for the men - yes, for the men, it was those very beautiful young Danish girls. Among those beautiful young Danish girls was Elna who enjoyed a popularity equal to any who came to enjoy the fellowship. Not only was Elna pretty, she was petite and the strong young men enjoyed swinging her high in the air in the folk dances that called for the lifting of the ladies. Even *lille Pete* could swing Elna high. Gunnar danced well and was often her partner. Most of the men had a turn to swing the new girl - a joy, to be sure, to a young lady who enjoyed life.

As the hour hand approached twelve, the crowd of young Danish immigrants thinned. The few autos that were there carried the late stayers off to a variety of communities: Metuchen, South River, Sayreville, New Brunswick - sometimes as far away as Newark and "the Elizabeths." What they shared in common vanished into the multi-ethnic communities wherein they had found their employment. Another week of struggle with language, custom and sometimes the inequities of the work place occupied their time. They looked forward to meeting again.

America Was to Be His Home

Travel was in his blood! As the son of a circus owner he had learned to travel - most of it in Denmark. From time to time the circus played in other countries on the continent of Europe, mostly in the major cities. As he grew in years, the adventure within him also grew and it was not long before he thought he should try traveling on his own.

He had learned to live in the cities of Europe, beginning with Copenhagen which was his home. Down at the harbor, which was not far from where he lived with his parents, he heard tall tales of other places in the world. The stories were, of course, embellished by the young seamen who wanted to impress all who would listen to their accounts of the attraction of world communities and of the young women who lived and worked in those distant places.

At twenty-one Carl Harald Olsen volunteered his services as a boiler assistant on one of the ocean going vessels headed for America. The work was hard. His hand never touched an oil can. Rather they took the shape of the shovels which had to be used to feed the boilers on board.

After nearly twenty days at sea in the hold of the ship, most of the crew were relieved of their ocean duties to stand at railside as the harbor tugs led the ship to its berth on the Delaware River where its cargo of merchandise was unloaded and weary passengers found their way to waiting friends and relatives who would help them find their way in the new land. Philadelphia appeared grander than it really was. The dim lights of the city flickered in the eyes of the young seaman who had yet to see the light of day in the vast dreamland called America.

Only a few days and nights in the Philadelphia port, still living on the vessel that had brought him there, convinced him that sailing was not the adventure in which he wanted to be permanently engaged, and he did what many before him had done: he jumped ship for better places and better circumstances in "this land of opportunity."

There were many Danes in Philadelphia, including members of Carl's family. These people had come a generation before and were well settled in the new land. They lived in neighborhoods that were not easily accessible from the industrial berths of ocean going vessels. Contact with them was almost non existent for Carl, and furthermore a young man on an adventure was not particularly interested in the settled life which was theirs.

24

The word soon came via the grapevine that the best opportunities for a young Danish lad, who was on an adventure, lay in the New York area where literally hundreds of recent immigrants had come, and notably for Carl, Danish immigrants. Perth Amboy, New Jersey, housed a large number of Danes from several waves of immigration from Denmark. What he found there was much more to his liking than the stuffiness of relatives, already having made good in the new land.

With his limited resources, Carl made his way to Essex County, New Jersey, which was only a stone's throw from New York City. It was not long before he found a job that matched his skills - strong hands and a strong back and a need for capital. Sam Fischer's brickyard had great need for those who could keep the brick-making ovens going through 24 hours each day.

The days were long. There was not much opportunity for social life, but when one is single and strong and adventuresome he finds time for social activity. *"Den danske Ungdomsforening"* (The Danish Young Peoples' Society) seemed like a logical place to find the excitement needed for another day of labor in the excruciating heat of the glowing furnaces.

The songs of renewal, both religious and secular, rang from the gathering places of these young people as they lifted their voice in one great big *"Skaal"* to their achievement in arriving in the new land. A few slept the next day away. The disciplined were hard at their labors again so they could enjoy yet another evening of celebrating and singing.

Thoughts of Denmark and thoughts of sea-going adventures soon evaporated as life evolved in the "new Denmark" of the Eastern seaboard. Most who came, including the young Carl Harald Olsen, did not return, but if and when those returns were made, they were not long lasting. America was to be their home.

A Summer Evening in Early July

The first Thursday in June of 1924 had been a very good day for Elna. Most days usually were. She had gotten up early to perform her kitchen duties and continued with her activity well past the noon hour. Inspite of the early hour of rising, Elna was ready for an evening at "the Hall." There she could again gather with her fellow Danes. America was a wonderful land; her employment was beyond anything that she could have hoped for. The knowledge that she had family in the area was comforting, but the camaraderie at "the Hall" gave the "plus" that made living in America the next best thing to being at home in her beloved Denmark.

Elna rode with August Hansen to Perth Amboy. He provided the transportation most times. When she arrived, she was not disappointed. Marie Petersen and Else Nissen, who were her two best friends in America, were there. Peter Rasmussen (*lille Pete*) was there as was Hans Rasmussen - not related to Peter. Jorgen Stensgaard with his lady friend, Elinor Begtrup, to whom he was engaged, was there. Anne, Sophie, Helene and Esther Helgesen soon arrived. In a very short time the Hall was filled. As the young people gathered, the musicians set a lively mood. Soon the dance floor was alive with rhythm and the walls echoed the songs that became a part of the evening.

In the far corner Christian Gravengaard and Folmer Rasmussen were engaged in animated discussion - surely about the inequities of the workplace. Evelyn and Hansine sat along the east wall expressing very clearly their joy in sharing whatever it was that they shared. Others moved about exchanging the trivia that was often exaggerated beyond the importance of its content.

Elna rarely lacked an invitation to dance, but now and again she needed to rest, to catch her breath. During one such moment that evening, her heart began to beat double time. She had glanced only momentarily to her right, but there, framed in the doorway to the Hall, stood a tall, handsome man. "Six-foot-two," he told her later. The measurement seemed inconsequential, when he shared it with her. What she knew in that first moment was that he was tall and clearly that he was handsome. She quickly framed a hope that he would enter the Hall and that he would ask her to dance.

As the evening progressed Elna seemed to require a good deal of "rest," placing her on the sidelines for the "right" invitation to dance. What Elna did not know as she formulated plans making herself available was that the tall and handsome man had already noticed her, not only as she sat "this one out," but also when she was engaged in a dance with one of the other men present. He liked what he saw, and soon he was before her inviting her to share with him in the rhythmic activity of the evening at the Hall in Perth Amboy.

He shared with her only that his name was Carl and that he had come up to the New York area from Philadelphia, where he had relatives. He had landed there only a few weeks before, but in the weeks that followed he learned that there were a lot of Danes in the New York metropolitan area and that there were greater opportunities for work there. He did not fail to tell her how pretty she was and how rhythmic her step and that, maybe, he would see her again one day.

The evening ended all too soon. It had been an exhilarating evening - a never-to-be-forgotten evening. It was an evening that was unlikely to occur again soon.

Elna departed with August with whom she had come to the Hall that evening, together with Holger Kirkegaard and Stine Gentorp, both of whom also lived in South River, not far from the Prentiss home.

Midsummer Dreaming

The summer days moved by quickly. It was the eve of *Sankt Hansdag*. The next day would mark the longest day of the year and a turning toward winter when everything seems harder, if it is not in fact. Getting down to the Hall in winter could be something of a chore and occasionally Thursday night got to be another quiet evening at home. But chatter about that did not last long among those assembled at the Hall on the eve of *Sankt Hansdag*. A lively schottish soon turned thoughts to the activity at hand.

But Elna was not thinking about the longest days of the year nor of winter evenings and the problems that they would present in getting to Perth Amboy. For her there was a lingering thought that centered around Carl's closing words the evening he appeared in the doorway of the Hall several weeks earlier. *"Vi mødes nok igen en gang."* [Perhaps we will meet again sometime.] It had been three weeks since Carl had added that thought to comments about Elna's beauty and rhythm on the dance floor. The thought had lingered from that time until now, but reality has a way of interrupting, and though the thought was intense, that evening the thought did not linger long. One cannot spend a lifetime or even an evening in mid-summer dreaming about someone who obviously has disappeared just as mysteriously as he had appeared. Who knows? He could have returned to Philadelphia - or maybe even Denmark. No more time and energy could be spent on the thought just now.

The evening, the eve of *Sankt Hansdag*, concluded sooner than had seemed possible. Elna returned to South River with August Hansen with whom she had ridden to Perth Amboy. Holger Kirkegaard and Stine Gentorp rode along as usual. Conversation was subdued. A good time was had by all, but there had been other times which had been more exhilarating than this terribly warm and steamy night "out on the town."

The following Thursday was a good deal more exciting - even in anticipation. The Fourth of July presented a good many of the young people with a day off. Conversation was vivid around what young Danes in America would do with that much time on their hands. Picnics, trips to New York, a swim at the beach or just time to reminisce. All of those thoughts and ideas were part of the chatter that evening at the *forsamling* [gathering] of young immigrant Danes.

28

The night was fairly young when a hush engulfed Elna's heart. In the doorway stood Carl. He was going to see her again, she thought. What a wonderful surprise! Would he still remember her? Or did he always whisper comments of interest into the ears of those with whom he danced? The questions raced through her mind with telegraphic speed - soon to be interrupted by an invitation to dance - yes, by Carl.

The dances with Carl were frequent that evening, and during each dance, he shared something of what had transpired for him in the intervening time between appearances at the gathering of the Danish Young People. He had been to New York. In Brooklyn there were other Danes. Among them, Carl thought, would surely be those who could help him find employment. The suggestions were many, but Carl had few skills that would make him readily employable in the "good paying" jobs. He tried the harbor area on the Hudson River. As a boiler assistant on one of the many ships that made port there, he could travel the world if nothing of interest should arise in America.

Argentina seemed like it might be a good destination. Thousands of Danes had settled there in Buenos Aires and adjacent communities. Danish ships came and went - some destined for the Far East. A trip around the world held some fascination in the search. From pier to pier he had inquired, but nothing seemed to be just right.

A quick trip to Bridgeport, Connecticut, ruled that city out. The Elizabeths and the Brunswicks of New Jersey held some promise, he told Elna. None of the above had worked out for him, but in Sayreville, New Jersey, there was an opportunity that could be temporary, if it did not work out to be satisfactory. The job was at Sam Fischer's Brickyard. Coal fired ovens needed to be tended around the clock, and as good fortune would have it, he landed a day job there. Also extremely to his liking and easy on his budget was free room and board which was part of the package. He could live right on the grounds of his employment granting a good deal of free time which otherwise would be spent in going to and from his employment. For now it was fine.

Carl sounded excited about what had developed for him. It also meant that he could attend the Thursday night activities at the Hall on a regular basis and he hoped that she would be there again. He liked her, he said. She was pretty, and there was a natural rhythm in her step which he thoroughly enjoyed, he added.

The Fall of 1924

There was a chill in the air. It was already mid to late September. The chill gave a hint of the short days and long nights that lay ahead. But the chill brought a briskness, not only to the air, but to the souls of young Danes who were beginning to enjoy their newfound land and the employment opportunities that were available to them.

Even though they enjoyed their jobs, they nevertheless struggled quite a bit with language, and with culture and ethics that sometimes violated their own sense of honesty and justice. Because of the limits of their vocabularies, they were hardpressed to insist on what they believed to be their rightful place in the work scheme of things. "Castigliano didn't deserve that job," someone would say. "No, that's right!" would come a comment, "but he's a friend of Antonio Zazzaro, and how are you going to get around that?" "Well, we'll work hard, and maybe there will come a break!" someone would say philosophically. And so the workday was spent, and there was much anticipation about the Thursday night gatherings where all of that could be discussed on a level playing field. "Vi er not dum Danes, etter all. Vi know sumting, but vi don't know the sumbuddy that kan giv us a lift!" they agreed.

The sharing of their experiences was the balm they needed - even before the first polka came that removed the feeling of the injustices that they were experiencing. Aching muscles soon gave way to renewed power - power to lift the young ladies which not only demonstrated their physical strength, but the strength that was in their souls.

It was the third Thursday of September when Carl showed up again at the Hall as he generally did. There was a glow on his face when he came through the entranceway to the dance floor. He scanned the sides of the room with their benches and was not disappointed in his search for Elna. There she sat on the east wall, looking especially prim, waiting for the moment that was at hand. Standing before Elna, he bowed politely, as he asked her for the next dance. In return Elna curtsied and joined him on the dance floor.

The tune had changed to a quiet waltz - an important change - because Carl had an idea to present. As it had turned out, the cook and housekeeper at Sam Fischer's Brickyard had resigned that very morning. When Carl learned the news, he went directly to Mr. Fischer to assure him that he knew just the lady that could take her place.

**Boarding House
Fischer Brickyard**

**Elna looks from a window of the boarding
house owned by the Fischer Brickyard.**

Could he present her name to Mr. Fischer, he asked Elna. Besides
being a good job, it would allow hours alone at the end of each day
for both of them where they could get better acquainted. Maybe
marriage would be out there in the not-too-distant future, Carl had
suggested. It would be perfect! Two incomes, free lodging (as singles
for now and newlyweds later on). With careful planning they could
maybe have a car, so that they could continue to have a social life at
the Hall on Thursdays and on Sunday afternoons in Old Bridge,
South River or Metuchen where large numbers of Danes had taken
up residence.

It all sounded wonderful to Elna, but experience had told her that
she should give something like that very serious thought before she
would agree to it. "You don't have to answer now!" Carl said to Elna.
"Hulda will be there until the end of the month! But maybe by next
Thursday you could give an answer," Carl continued. "That would be
time enough!" he thought.

The chemistry of love went into high gear. Fleeting thoughts of
returning to Denmark, which now were not as intense as they had been,

31

Carl Harold Olsen	The wedding day
at the Fischer Brickyard	of Carl H. Olsens
where he worked	& Elna J. Laumark

danced in and out of Elna's mind all evening. The handsome charm of this "worldly" Dane with whom she was dancing, and being held tight, moved in and out with what seemed like growing intensity. Elna's practical mind worked hard with the idea of two incomes, a readymade place of residence and the possibilities of establishing a new life in America. With whom should she consult. While she had consulted often with the younger sister that she had escorted to the United States, the matter that she was now entertaining was of such significance that maybe the advice of this younger sister would not contain the elements of experience that were required.

Had the music stopped with abruptness, or did it just seem that way? In any event the evening was over, and each was to return to his or her place of residence and gainful employment. Elna had given her promise that she would have an answer next Thursday. "That would be O.K." Carl said.

The ride home with August, Holger and Stine was very quiet. Each mused about the evening which had been theirs.

Two Promises Fulfilled

It had been clear to Edwin Prentiss that his "little Elna" was in love. The observation had been confirmed by Helga Petersson, his long-time cook with whom Elna had been working for nearly two years. It came as no surprise when Elna appeared before him with her announcement of a possible job change, nor was it a surprise that she asked if she could leave as early as October 1 should the new job opportunity be available to her. In fact, it was clear to all that Elna was marriage-bound. Under the circumstances, Edwin Prentiss had already discussed the matter with Helga Petersson who thought she could handle things to make an early departure possible.

At Sam Fischer's Brickyard, Carl had been busy paving the way for Elna and had convinced the Fischers that Elna would be available to start the day following Hulda's last day in the kitchen at the brickyard residence.

The week that intervened between the third and fourth Thursdays of September - the week in which Elna had promised that she would arrive with an answer to Carl's suggestion that she come to work at the boarding house on the grounds of Sam Fischer's Brickyard flew by. Carl, who usually arrived late at the Danish Young People's meetings, was early on that last Thursday. He had arrived early so that he could hear the "yes" that he anticipated and so that he could then go to a telephone to report Elna's willingness to work at the Sayreville brickyard and to report that she could begin on October 1.

Because time was of an essence in all of this, Sam Fischer had prevailed on Hulda to stay for a couple of days to give "the new girl" some counsel on the duties at the boarding house. Because of Elna's quick wit, Hulda found the training sessions to be a joy. At the end of the two days of training, Hulda reported to Mr. Fischer that she was certain that things would go without a hitch, and, so they did where the work was concerned.

Things did go without any great hitches, but duties at the boarding house turned out to be quite a different experience from that of Elna's experience at the Prentiss home. Among the differences was the absence of one who could translate or interpret what was being requested - all of which was complicated by the multiplicity of languages which served as the springboard from which English was learned. When Castigliano ventured into English from his native Italian, the English words did not sound like they did when Yedziniak said the same words from his Polish background, and to Danish ears

33

Carl and Elna Olsen with Harold

any, and all, of the English that was spoken at the boarding house sounded foreign. The dialects provided an English that was unique. At best the English that was spoken at any time was a comedy and an occasion from which much discussion arose about what was being said.

Life at Sam Fischer's Brickyard was not all work nor was it a constant scene of language confusion. There was time for two people in love to talk in a language which they shared from their native Denmark. They talked about their dreams for marriage and a whole new life in America. The dreams about which they talked turned into reality with the speed of the new economic reality for which their work provided. Marriage plans were made quickly. The pastor at St. Stephen's Church in Perth Amboy was contacted, and it was agreed that November 29, 1924 could be the date for the wedding.

The place of the wedding was to be Sam Fischer's Boarding House, and strong backs and hands prepared the living room for the occasion. The bride was dressed in a flowing brown paisley dress. The groom stood tall in a deep brown suit, the only suit that he owned. On the evening of November 29, Carl Harald Olsen and Elna Jespersen Laumark appeared before Pastor Hans O. Jensen to exchange their vows. Elna's sister, Christine Jespersen Laumark, served as the bridesmaid and Aksel Jensen, Carl's friend, served as best man. The bride and groom were both too practical for much fanfare, so there was little of that, including any thought of a honeymoon.

The only honeymoon was the love that radiated from each of them as they said their vows and the assurance that they would do well in their new life. They had each other. They had an address at their place of employment and there would be an opportunity to put a little aside for another day sometime in the future.

34

Brick, Barges and Baby

The Samuel K. Fischer Brickyard fronted on the Raritan River, a river filled with human waste and industrial debris. Its color was brick red in whatever shade of red one would care to choose. At the brickyard's edge the Raritan River responded to the tides of the Atlantic Ocean, making it stagnant rather than flowing. The smell was that of a mixture of decaying garbage and oil ladened metal shavings and chips. One could live by that river but not live in it. An occasional rodent managed to paddle its way through the foam which often formed on the surface of the water, but fish did poorly, if at all, in its polluted waters.

The Raritan River served as the delivery channel for the clay products that were manufactured at Sam Fischer's Brickyard. Barge-like platforms were moored to a pier which ran alongside the brickyard's edge. As the barge platforms dipped into the river under the heavy load of bricks and other kiln-fired clay, they were towed away by barges that billowed columns of black smoke into the air. Rarely did the smoke go very far. It was blanketed by fog for most of the night and many of the waking hours - especially in the winter when nighttime lasted longer than the daylight hours.

Through the thick fog and stench came the sounds of the eerie foghorns, as if speaking to other horns of moving traffic on the industrial highway of the sea. If one listened carefully, one could hear the bell, or bells, of the sea markers that dotted the harbor waterways. "Red on the right on the return," assured the captains that they were going up stream as long as the red buoys were on their starboard side.

The land side of Sam Fischer's Brickyard was marked by a railroad spur of the Pennsylvania Railroad. On that brief bit of railroad came the clay and other materials needed for the manufacture of brick and building materials. One could hear the steam engines - billowing smoke into the air - chug their way into the siding and, with an arresting sound, spew their excess steam into the day or night. When windows were open in the one residence at the brickyard in the summertime, it sounded like the steam engine was right in the house.

Dropping off the cars and reordering them for departure brought the usual thump of hopper cars mating each other for a journey into the industrial world of metropolitan New York. The engineer always gave a long toot on the whistle and a few short ones as he left the brickyard for destinations that only the engineer knew.

For the newly married couple, Carl and Elna Olsen, this was home. Winter soon came and went. Carl continued with the long hours of shoveling coal into the brick ovens at Sam Fischer's, and Elna, the new employee and the new bride at Sam Fischer's brickyard, added her zest for life and her domestic skills to maintaining a rooming and boarding house in better condition than it had known for some time. The smells, the noises, the pollution went relatively unnoticed for the young couple as they started out on a new life together.

With the second winter came some relief from the long hours of work. Construction in the metropolitan area of New York experienced the same curtailment that building in other places experienced during winter. The opportunities for attending meetings of the Danish Young People were again possible, but with the beginning of that second winter, the early summer discovery that Elna was pregnant did not always favor a trip to Perth Amboy for the fun and fellowship that had been enjoyed there at an earlier time. The usual morning sickness had not been present for Elna, but the weight of a growing child within her womb, coupled with the rigorous work at the rooming house, sometimes necessitated absence from the Thursday evening meetings of the Danish Young People's Society.

In December the nights became especially long. Christmas was coming and thoughts of Laumark and Denmark fleetingly visited the pregnant young lady as she thought about the holidays in Denmark, and now her Christmas here in America. A child was coming, her own child. Thoughts about this new life occurred with growing frequency each day. How soon the child was to be born was not clear, but December passed, and on January 3, 1926, a son, Harold Edwin Olsen, was born.

German and Italian laborers at Sam Fischer's Brickyard, as well as the Irish and Yugoslavian workers, who normally were "macho men" looked on with interest at this exciting event in their midst. Their language, which often was quite earthy, took on a reserved quality. New life excited them, and they often shared the wish with Carl and Elna that life would be good to this newborn in their midst. If they prayed for him, that was not evident, but clearly there was awe and respect for the newborn child at Sam Fischer's Brickyard.

From New Jersey
to
New England

From New Jersey to New England

Haze - industrial haze - hung low over Sayreville, New Jersey, in August of 1926, as it had since late June of that year. And while the whole earth appeared to be shaded by that haze, the heat of the sun penetrated the haze quite successfully and converted every square inch of the earth into an oven. Upper 90s could often be classified as a cool day where the temperature often went over 100 degrees in the early weeks of September. An occasional "Noreaster" broke the pattern but only for very brief spells. One could only count on one or two such spells for the summer.

It was on an evening of one of the cool spells that Carl and Elna took time to talk about destinies, their own in particular. With their baby, Harold, now almost seven months of age, it became clear that Sam Fischer's Brickyard was not a place to raise a family. The concern was heightened by the knowledge that Elna was due for another child in April of the next year. Though Harold had not been a fussy baby, it was clear that the heat bothered him as it did the adults who had already done their growing up and were now hard at work in one of the hottest locations in the industrial complex that made up greater New York.

Jacob Norregaard, who had been present at one of the meetings of the Danish Young People in Perth Amboy, had told the group of better opportunities in the much cleaner community of Hartford, Connecticut. In addition, Norregaard had told the group that the Danish Young Peoples Society in Hartford had just purchased a retreat center in nearby Unionville where Danes could gather to enjoy nature's beauty and breezes and her babbling brooks. *Vennelejr*, as the retreat center had been named, could be reached easily by bus from anywhere in Hartford. Niels Lund had been enlisted as a regular fiddle player for dancing and singing each weekend. And Bertine Norregaard, who was something of an expert at Danish folk dancing, would lead the group on Friday and Saturday evening as the various visitors might desire. High also on the list was a reading room where the music of song birds and rummaging squirrels would provide the background for deep meditation and reflection. Buzzing bees and the aroma of the flowers that the bees had visited would also provide for qualities of life that could not, and did not, survive the smog filled atmosphere of the world's largest harbor and its attendant industries.

As Carl and Elna talked, what Norregaard had shared with them that evening loomed large in the conversation about destinies and importantly their own destiny as a young family determined to make it in this new land to which they had come. "A bit of Denmark" was what Norregaard had offered them - something for which they longed with ever deeper longing as the realities of their new life pressed upon them.

They decided Carl would go to Perth Amboy to arrange for a move to Hartford, Connecticut. Surely there would be someone at one of the meetings who could take Carl and Elna and their son, Harold, to Perth Amboy for the all-day bus ride to Hartford, Connecticut. Per chance, Carl could also make arrangements with someone there to make it possible to have needed food and shelter upon their arrival in the New England city. Carl was not disappointed in his quest. As it turned out the arrangements were made on Carl's first visit to the Hall in which the young Danes met in Perth Amboy each Thursday.

The bus ride itself to Hartford took only five and one half hours, but with transfers and stops along the way, the trip took thirteen hours. It took two hours and fifteen minutes to ride in the old REO Greyhound bus to New York. The bus departed daily at 6:00 a.m. for the Port Authority Building on the west side of Manhattan - a distance of about 28 miles. With safe arrival there, it was another 50 minutes to the East Side Bus Terminal for a connection with a bus destined for Hartford. Inbound buses were often late for literally hundreds of reasons, but after nearly four hours in transit from Perth Amboy, Carl, Elna and Harold were safely aboard the bus destined for Hartford with arrival time scheduled for 7:00 p.m. in downtown Hartford.

Carl had been advised, however, that he could ask the busdriver to let them off at the corner of Fairfield and Maple Avenues where Jens Tonnesen would meet them for a short eight-block ride to a third-floor, one-room apartment "which should keep you until you find a better place a little later on." Traffic throughout southern Connecticut seemed unusually heavy - especially as they got closer to the late afternoon rush hour. Traffic signals punctuated the "Boston Post Road" from New York to New Haven, Connecticut - one about every three blocks on average, necessitating frequent stops. Each stop with its commensurate "hiss" from the bus' airbrakes and its grinding of gears - one through six - made the trip even more wearing than they had envisioned. Apprehension about the anticipated hospitality of a previously unmet Jens Tonnesen added to the burden of the journey.

With great forethought Elna had remembered to pack some waxed paper to take care of the inevitable diaper changes that would take place for Harold. This relieved them of some of the most offensive smells, but not all of the traveling parents had been so thoughtful. The smell of dirty diapers - some of which remained on crying children - filled the bus, and by arrival time in the city of Hartford the bus was ripe with the smell of human exhaust and the sounds of human exhaustion. When the bus driver called out "Maple and Fairfield," further declaring that the exit from the bus was "this way out," Elna and Carl (and Harold who was sleeping soundly by then) were ready for departure into the fresh air of the capital and "park city" of Hartford, Connecticut.

Young and hearty, the three arriving passengers stepped from the bus, tired but rejoicing. Jens Tonnesen was there as he had promised. *"Velkommen til vor by! Vi er glade fordi i kom!"* said Jens.

Putnam Street, Hartford, Connecticut

40

Hartford, The Park City and Its Neighborhoods

Hartford - the "Park City"

The third-floor, one-room apartment, "which should keep you until you find a better place a little later on, " was clean and well appointed. A double bed stood against the east wall. A little kitchen table (for two) sat under twin, double hung windows to the south. The windows were draped with white sheer curtains which hardly moved inspite of the fact that the windows were open. There was little breeze that came through the windows that evening. A two burner gas stove sat on a counter which ran the length of the west wall. Above the counter was a double doored cabinet which contained a few dishes which had been gathered up over a period of years (there were no matching items.) Just to the north of the double bed was a little rocking chair. On the north wall, with just enough room to pass by the bed to the rocker, stood a handmade, but adequate, closet for an item or two of clothing. Between the closet and the kitchen counter there was just enough space for two small suitcases. The bathroom was "down the hall" and "it is shared by two men who are gone before six in the morning." "You should get along quite well," said the landlord.

Carl and Elna did not have time or inclination to assess the adequacy of the apartment for them "until they could find something better." They were glad to have a place to lie down and to take care of Harold who needed to be cleaned up from the long bus ride from Sayreville, New Jersey. And inspite of the noise of city buses which stopped on the street below, every ten minutes, they slept soundly - as soundly as one can sleep under the attack of mosquitoes that worked diligently throughout the night.

The next morning Carl and Elna discovered that their third-floor apartment at 401 New Britain Avenue was located over a little neighborhood store that carried almost everything that young families needed - oatmeal, milk, eggs, salami, hard rolls and butter, pulverized coffee and *The Hartford Courant*. While food was first on the agenda for the day, the search for a job was second, and *The Hartford Courant* provided assistance with the latter.

Elna, whose English was much improved over the first few weeks of her residency in the U.S.A., slipped down the stairs to view the staples and dairy products which she needed to make a little breakfast for the three of them. She fared well and was soon busy trying to make her "new" stove work and to think of a way to preserve items which needed cool temperatures. At the same time Elna attended to Harold who still

42

needed special attention and whose food still needed special preparation.

A quick look at the Want Ads made it clear that there were plenty of jobs available in Hartford. Not only was Hartford the "Park City," it was the home of hundreds of factories that could use both skilled and unskilled labor. Among them were Hartford Steam Boiler, Hartford Machine Screw Company, Underwood Typewriter, Royal Typewriter, Colt Manufacturing, Arrow, Hart and Heggeman, Stanley Works (in New Britain and accessible by The Connecticut Company bus line), Hartford Electric Light Co., Pratt and Whitney Aircraft, and Hamilton Standard Propeller. Among the cleaner jobs were positions at Aetna Life Insurance Company and Traveler's Insurance Company and as good fortune would have it - two dairy companies owned and operated by Danes. Emil Godiksen was a co-owner of the Lincoln Dairy, and A. C. Petersen owned and operated A. C. Petersen Farms and was experimenting with a dairy store on Park Street where one could get ice cream - "the best ever." These companies and others of a smaller scale were all within walking distance of 401 New Britain Avenue - a long walk in some instances, but not out of reach on foot.

Normally October 1 provided "air conditioning" but this day, day one at the third-floor apartment at 401, was unbearable. With temperatures in the high 80s and no breeze, the third-floor apartment (just under the roof) seemed more like an oven than a place of residence. And unlike many apartment buildings, there was no porch on this one. The porch had given way to the neighborhood store which occupied the first floor. Elna did her best to keep Harold in the shade at nearby bus stops and/or mini-parks - not venturing far from 401 which inspite of its heat provided some safety in the "new" city for her and her young child.

Day one was also a hot one for Carl who spent the day going from factory to factory in search of work that would keep him and his family at 401. With many stops along the way, Carl - before the day was over - got a job doing what he was good at (he had no apprentice skills) at Hartford Steam Boiler. Beginning at 7:00 a.m. Monday morning, October 4, Carl was hard at work in the boiler room of Hartford Steam Boiler, firing the furnaces that kept the machinery going in that factory. The walk from 401 New Britain Avenue to Capitol Avenue in near downtown Hartford was over a mile in distance. Clearly breakfast came early - and especially on this first day of work - since the apartment felt like an oven through much of the night which kept the three who had slept well the night before tossing and turning throughout the night.

In bed that night the talk was brief in spite of the restlessness. There were no long paragraphs about how each spent the day, only the necessary exchange to reiterate that they now had a place to stay "until they could find something better" and they now had employment which over time should make it possible to improve their lot in the "much cleaner" and "park city" of Hartford, Connecticut.

One-Hundred-and-Twenty-Seven Grandview Terrace

By mid-October the weather in the "park city" of Hartford had returned to normal. Most days were sunny, and the wind was blustery. Dust curled in the street gutters as did some of the leaves which had already begun to fall. In the distant Avon Mountains there were tinges of red and orange and yellow as maple trees began to yield to winter. Some trees displayed deep brown while others punctuated the woods with varying shades of white to golden yellow. Birds of every description gathered in the sky and swirled in formation for the trip south - many to the mid-Atlantic States Estuary marked most clearly by Chesapeake Bay. Others prepared for the much longer trip to the southern states of Georgia and Florida.

By mid-October it was already clear that "the third-floor one-room apartment that would keep them until they found something better" was far too small for a family of three with "one on the way."

Carl had not had too much time to look around. With a work schedule of 7:00 a.m. to 5:00 p.m. daily and with over a mile to walk each way, there was little time to look around. By October the sun did not reach the streets of Hartford until 7:30 a.m., and by the same hour in the evening it was already setting in the west. If there were any nice places, they would not be as evident in the darkness as in the light.

Elna's schedule was a bit better. After the normal morning household chores she could, on a clear fall day, explore the neighborhood. Traffic on New Britain Avenue, which was never very heavy, lightened to a passing automobile every now and then. Horse-drawn vehicles carrying produce, ice and an occasional delivery from G. Fox & Co could be heard and seen clopping their way through the neighborhoods. The ice-man could be heard announcing his presence so that those who needed ice would sound their, "Yoo Hoo," out their third or fourth or fifth-floor windows. (A few efficient, or absent tenants, remembered to put their "Ice Card" in the window, turned to indicate the size cut they desired). The "rag-man" - usually with an old nag - sang his daily song - "Cash paid for rags." The Connecticut Company buses sent up their usual columns of smoke as they left the curbsides where they had come to a halt with the hissing of airbrakes to discharge and receive passengers. There was always something to look at.

Elna, of course, looked at the activity and nodded a pleasant "Hello" from time to time to passing women with their shopping bags or dawdling youngsters who seemed always to be a half-block behind. But

Elna's assignment was to look around the neighborhood for a nice place where a family of four could live with some degree of comfort - exceeding certainly what they lived in at the moment. After several trips throughout the neighborhood - taking a different street each time - she found what she thought would be a good place for Carl and her and the children It had a small backyard where one could spread a blanket for an "at home" picnic and the drinking up of whatever sunshine would be available. One-hundred-twenty-seven Grandview Terrace was only four blocks away from 401 New Britain Avenue - an easy walk for Carl when he got home from work at about 1:00 p.m. on Saturday.

To Elna's surprise she occasionally heard Danish on the street. It should not have been a surprise. Jens Tonnesen, who had met them at the bus, had shared with them that he lived in the neighborhood. He had even mentioned that there were "a few Danes living here," but Elna had forgotten that. With a smile on her face, she ran a little to catch up to greet two ladies who were "busy at it" with their "clipped" Copenhagen Danish - a language with which she had become familiar in her days in Denmark's capital city. A bit surprised, the ladies were pleased to meet another Dane, and they welcomed her with a brief conversation.

When Elna asked if there was a Danish Church in the city, they assured her that there was one, but it was not close. "We hardly ever go there!" they said to her. "It's down on Russ and Babcock Street," they said with one voice, sure that Elna knew exactly where that was. "But there is another place," they said. "It's the White Street Hall, and that is closer. The Danish Brotherhood and Sisterhood meet there." "And, if I am not mistaken," said one, "the Danes own it." "It's over on White Street," said the other, again sure that Elna knew where that was too.

When Elna shared her findings with Carl that day, he assured her that there was a Danish Church - "down there on Russ and Babcock Streets." He had walked by it one day when he had taken a "new street" on his way home. "There are a lot of churches down in that part of town," he said. But he had noticed this one because there was a sign in the yard that said: *"Vor Frelsers Evangelisk-Lutherske Kirke - Gudstjeneste hver Søndag kl. 10:30"* (Our Savior's Evangelical Lutheran Church - Worship every Sunday at 10:30). He also indicated that on Saturday they could go over to look at 127 Grandview Terrace, if somebody else had not rented it by then. He was sure that they could afford the $17.00 a month that was being asked for it. He had been told at work that he soon would get a raise to $.35 an hour from the $.32 he was getting now. "You're a good worker - and strong. You're just what we need!" they had included with the announcement of the raise.

A Changing Neighborhood

One-hundred-twenty-seven Grandview Terrace had been an elegant home when it was built in the 1870s. The two-story house provided for gracious living quarters on the main floor with bedrooms and a bath occupying the upper level. Two fire places on the main floor provided heat for the whole house on cold winter days, and exposure to blowing breezes provided for relief from the hot, and often sticky, days of summer. A magnificent gas jet chandelier adorned the dining room with each of the other rooms equipped with at least one jet for illumination during the nighttime hours.

Located, as it was, on a major ridge extending from near downtown Hartford to the southwestern border of Wethersfield, the view was spectacular from a front room balcony. The Connecticut River could be viewed from that balcony with commercial river traffic providing most of the interest. To the west was a deck that covered much of the kitchen portion of the house. From that deck the Avon mountains showed off their color with the seasonal changes. It was clear that once, only the "very well-off" people could have lived there.

In 1926, approximately 50 years later, "one-twenty-seven" was in a changing neighborhood. The house itself had been changed to become a two-family residence. With the residual wealth still nearby, the immigrant newcomers dotted the neighborhood, making a patchwork quilt of human existence. The neighborhood was not dangerous generally speaking, but people were uneasy about the changes taking place. Single family homes were now becoming apartments. And, yes, Elna had heard Danish on occasion as she went out, but she was more apt to hear some other foreign tongue as she went about her domestic duties. A block or two made all the difference in the world as to whether the language would be English or some other language from the continent of Europe.

Carl, Elna and Harold learned to live there in their three-room, first-floor apartment. The kitchen was just large enough so that all of the meals could be eaten there. The dining room with its majestic chandelier made a splendid activities room, with the front room as bedroom. A pantry off the kitchen had been converted to a bathroom which was adequate for the family. It was an awkward situation when company came - they had to pass through the bedroom to reach the activities room - but with their newness in the community Carl and Elna did not have a great deal of company anyway. It was a big improvement

48

over 104 New Britain Avenue. It was the next step to a better life about which they both dreamed.

The winter months ahead dimmed the enthusiasm of the Olsen family from time to time. Carl's work was not much farther away than it had been in the "make do" one-room apartment, but winter could occasionally deal a severe storm, making the walk especially from work a very taxing kind of walk. Some days it seemed that in taking one step forward there was a sliding of two steps back. Here and there, there was a car stuck in the snow and a "helping hand" was needed. Now and again there was an elderly woman or man trying to get groceries home safely. Sometimes a child could be seen standing in a doorway with no one to open the door for him to get out of the cold. The crispness of the early morning walk was often invigorating, but the walk home after having worked hard in the super-heated boiler room at the factory made the trip home almost always a difficult journey.

The hours at home for Elna were often very long. Harold was good company most of the time, but Elna longed for adults with whom to share. She had not yet had an opportunity to worship at *Vor Frelsers Kirke* or to visit with anyone who belonged there. Socializing for one who enjoyed being with people was extremely limited. A few of the neighbors seemed very nice, but language and apprehension were often barriers to communication. "Use the dictionary," she was often told when she complained about the new language as not being adequate for her socializing needs - to which she often replied, "That's fine, if you know how to spell the words!" Her mid-term pregnancy didn't help either - especially on those days when the snow was sixteen to eighteen inches deep.

Eager to get out of the house, the occasion came for Elna in an unusual manner. The day had been an especially long one on Tuesday, December 14. Carl left for work early as usual. Harold had been whimpering throughout the night. In the morning it was clear that he was coming down with something. As the day progressed, Harold's temperature "went off the charts." It seemed like an eternity before Carl arrived - especially exhausted. The weather had not been especially bad. There were only traces of snow here and there from an earlier snowstorm, but the day had been difficult at work, he said. The sight of a very tired husband coupled with the anxiety over a sick child gave her impetus to leave the house for consultation with the nearby pharmacist. A bit apprehensive about being out in the darkness in a neighborhood which was still new to her, Elna nevertheless set out to handle a rather simple chore - a twofold task which gave her opportunity to get outside and also to do something about Harold's illness.

The evening out proved to be more of an adventure than she had planned The story as she told it to Carl who was oblivious to difficulties outside the house was that she had been attacked from behind. "I wrestled myself free," she said, "but," pointing to her bleeding chest, "I have been cut here. The man ran! He ran that way," she said, filled with panic. The cut turned out to be superficial. The wound inflicted to her psyche was of greater significance. With fear always hovering in her soul after that experience, Elna was apprehensive about the changes taking place in the neighborhood of which she had not been very keenly aware.

Inspite of the challenges, the new life was better than life at Sam Fischer's Brickyard had been or that had been envisioned for a growing young son there. Elna thanked God often and looked forward to the day when she could do so in the house of God on the corner of Russ and Babcock Street near downtown Hartford.

New Environs Become Familiar

Out of necessity Carl arose early every morning. The coal-fired kitchen stove was first on the agenda. The grates needed turning. The banked coals, now ashes, needed removal and a new supply of coal needed to be procured. There was, of course, a quick face washing and shaving that needed doing. And breakfast - he did not need to prepare it, but he did need to eat it. And, oh yes, a lunch to remember. (Elna prepared it as she prepared the morning breakfast). It was a long walk to work - a mile and one half - Carl estimated. To be at work a little before seven Carl needed to leave the house at 6:20 a.m. at the latest. The wake-up time to accomplish all of the morning chores that were required was 5:15 a.m., sometimes as late as 5:30 a.m., but always early.

Carl took the "Zion Street Route," as he called it. Across New Britain Avenue, he took a jog to the left and then to the right where Hughes Street intersects with Zion Street. When he had walked about another 15 blocks, he took a right to Putnam Street and another right to Babcock Street where a left turn took him nearly to the front door of his place of employment on Capitol Avenue. The whole journey was 22 blocks and included passing a number of neighborhood grocery stores, two pharmacies, three dry goods stores, a Kresge's Department Store, the "Economy" store, and a minimum of twelve taverns or "beer joints" as they were called.

The big church on the corner of Park and Putnam Streets was St. Anne's Catholic Church (The French Church) and the two churches on opposite corners of Russ and Babcock Streets were Lutheran - "The German Church" and "The Danish Church" (*Vor Frelsers Kirke*). The house across Putnam Street from St. Anne's Church was the residence for the five and sometimes six priests who conducted mass daily for French Canadians and other French speaking people. The first house on the left going north on Putnam Street housed the "sisters" who taught catechism at the parochial grade school next to the parish church.

All along the way to work were other workers intent on arriving on time at their respective places in the factories that surrounded the neighborhood which was locally called "Frog Hollow" - because the dominant population was French? or because the Hog River (actually the Park River) flowed through the neighborhood and was the home of a variety of sturdy amphibian life (frogs included)? No one really knew.

As Carl began his journey to the Hartford Steam Boiler plant, he always nodded politely at others going to or coming from work -

51

knowing that *"God Dag"* would not work as a greeting. By the time Carl had reached Zion Hill Cemetery, about twelve or thirteen blocks from home on the east side of the street, he had teamed up with one or two who worked at Underwood Typewriter Company, Hartford Machine Tool, Arrow, Hart and Heggeman or some other factory just west of the intersection of Capitol Avenue where it crosses Broad Street. From these men Carl learned to know the community. Among the things that he learned was that on Ward Place there was a dairy called "The Lincoln Dairy" owned by Danes, Godiksen and Arendsen, the men thought. "They must live around here someplace," someone volunteered. Carl also learned something of the housing which was close to where he worked, all the time thinking that the walk, while invigorating, was nevertheless a long one, especially after a long and tedious day (often ten and sometimes twelve hours), and now in the winter, in the dark both ways. In only a few days he knew the names of all of the streets he walked on and those he crossed and those he went by, and saying those street names as he walked on or by them helped him with the monotony of it all.

At Grandview Terrace, Elna carried on with what she had to work with. Besides planning Danish meals and creating delectable Danish pastry, Elna repaired clothing; it needed to last as long as it could. When she got an extra piece of cloth , either from a discarded garment or from a bargain purchase at "Mr. Spain's Cloth and Clothing Store," she made something for herself or for Harold, who was now crawling vigorously throughout the house. As she cooked and as she sewed, favorite songs passed through her head and, on occasion, took on audible sounds. Among her favorites was *"Nu falmer Skoven trindt om Land,"* a beautiful song of fall's display, by N.F.S. Grundtvig and especially appropriate for the lateness of the year. When the morning was especially crisp and bright, she sang *"Den signede Dag med Fryd vi ser af Havet til os opkomme"* and *"I Østen stiger solen op,"* one of B. S. Ingeman's best, she thought. These two latter songs addressed the beauty of the dawning day and its beautiful sunrises.

Harold was thrilled by musical exchanges with his mother. If for any reason he was not quite up to par, Elna liked to sing *"Lille Guds Barn, hvad skader dig?"* (God's Little Child, What Troubles You?) a Grundtvig hymn which addressed God's watchfulness over his children. The confidence with which she sang assured Harold of God's love, but also of the love of his mother. While both Elna and Harold waited for Carl's return in the late afternoon, it was *"I en kælder, sort som Kul, aller dybest*

52

nede, var et prægtigt Musehul og en Muserede." (Down in the Cellar Is a Magnificent Mouse Hole with a Very Lively Family) While Harold did not fully understand the story in that song, he seemed to be especially amused by the words that spoke of mice that did not have to wash up after meals. The bedtime songs always included *"Den lille Ole med Paraplyen"* (The Little Ole with His Umbrella).

Inspite of some days of grave concern about the new life in Hartford, Carl, Elna and Harold settled in. The absence of grandparents, siblings, or very many close friends made for some long days and especially evenings, but life was better for them than it had been at the very dirty and difficult work at Sam Fischer's Brickyard in Sayreville, New Jersey. Springtime held great promise, especially because of the anticipated arrival of a second child. "Hopefully, a girl this time," Elna whispered quietly to herself.

A Familiar , but Foreign, Neighborhood

Harold was an early riser, but occasionally he was still asleep long after his father, Carl, was off to work. On those occasions Elna used the time to jot down notes for her weekly letter to Denmark, always written on Friday, even if it meant getting up earlier than usual or remaining up later than usual. It was the weekly letters to and from Denmark that sustained her. Everything she knew about living her day-to-day life was imported from Denmark, in treasured memories; she had very few items which she had brought with her as reminders of her roots.

As Elna wrote the notes for inclusion in her weekly letter, she thought about each one she had left behind in 1922 when she set sail for America. As much as anyone Elna missed her eldest brother, Viggo, who was next in line after her in the birth sequence of nine children. In disposition Viggo was much like Elna, who had always had a good sense of humor and who enjoyed life. Like Elna, he was also the story-teller. "He could make a stick come alive," it was often said about him as he spun one yarn after another, especially if it had to do with hunting and fishing. When Viggo helped his father with the farm work, he often flushed up a bevy of quail and somehow in the telling the number became nearly astronomical.

But there were also Martin and Karna, who were close enough in years to be thought of as twins. She did not long for them as she did Viggo, but she missed them nevertheless. Christine, who had traveled with Elna on the pioneer journey to America, also came to mind. She had left that sister in New Jersey with family members there, and she wondered about her. While there were letters from Christine, they did not arrive weekly, so concern sometimes grew about the now twenty-one- year-old girl.

But Elna's social life was not entirely limited to the paper exchanges with her family members. There were the neighbors on Grandview Terrace, though she did not see them often and sometimes had difficulty communicating with them. English, with a Polish accent or a Turkish one, was as difficult for Elna as Elna's English with a Danish accent was for them. But each time they met, they exchanged something - a concern, a recipe, a cooking utensil or whatever immigrant families had to share with each other.

On occasion a Danish couple came to visit. (It was not always Sundays that were available to foreigners to do their socializing.) Sven and Anna Peterson were fairly frequent visitors, because Sven had a car.

Oh, it was not his car, but as the butler for one of Hartford's more successful families he was often allowed to take the car so that he could take Anna "out for a spin" - usually on Thursdays which was also Anna's day off. (Anna worked as cook at the Reynolds house where Sven served as butler.)

If Sven and Anna promised to come right back to work after church (2:30 or 3:00 in the afternoon), they were also allowed to take the car for that outing. From time to time Sven and Anna stopped by to take Carl, Elna and Harold to church at *Vor Frelsers Kirke* at Russ and Babcock Streets, the church that Carl passed almost daily on his way to work.

At *Vor Frelsers Kirke* Carl and Elna met other Danes, most of whom were recent immigrants from all over the Kingdom of Denmark. Though the congregation had been established in 1883, it had served as something of a revolving door in sending Danish families into the new world in which they were to live. The Peter Rasks, the Anders Madsens and the Jens Christensens were the only remaining families from the congregation established in the 80s to meet the worship and social needs of adventuresome Danish couples and singles, most of whom at Carl and Elna's time were those who came in the 20s of the twentieth century. With Pastor Henning Lund-Sorensen, who had been called from Denmark, English did not fare well in meetings of the congregation - whether for worship or for *aarsmødet* (annual meeting) or other purposes of the congregation. It mattered not. The congregation was there to serve Danes.

Social life for Elna centered pretty much in home and church. Such was not so for Carl. The daily walk to work put him in another social world. The man with whom he walked and talked the most on the way to work was John Kiczuk, a Lithuanian, who attended Sts. Cyril and Methodius Church only blocks from the Danish Church. Vernon Tibodeau joined in fairly soon after Carl met John. He shared that his family was quite regular in both confession and attendance at mass at St. Patrick's Church - an Irish parish where his French origins were only tolerated for religious purposes. George Swedburg didn't attend church, but if he were to go to one, it would be the big Swedish Church on the corner of Capital Avenue and Broad Streets. "Hulteen," he thought the minister's name was. Gil Kavitsky was usually out of sorts with a hangover from having played cards at Ben's Bar the night before. "We drank only a few beers," he assured his companions. Somehow Gil always smelled like the smells that emanated from the numerous beer joints punctuating Carl's journey to the Hartford Steam Boiler factory.

With that kind of exposure to the new world, Carl was glad to go to church where some of the old world provided for a more familiar experience. "You kan, ov course, overdo dat Church ting," he would often explain to his Danish friends, many of whom could identify with the observation.

Shared social life sometimes took Carl and Elna to the White Street Hall which was much closer to home than the church. "White Street" as the hall came to be called had been purchased by the Danish Brotherhood, because "it was available, it was 'cheep' and 'der ver still sum Daenz that livet arroundt der'!" The social life at White Street was quite different from that which was lived at *Vor Frelsers Kirke,* but it served, as did the church, an important purpose for a people who had just been tossed by fate or deliberate decision into a pluralistic and ethnic European society that had gathered in Frog Hollow and/or adjacent neighborhoods.

The neighborhood was becoming familiar, but in more ways than one it was a "foreign" neighborhood. Carl, Elna and Harold were in a new world, in many worlds, in Hartford, Connecticut - "Downtown where the jobs are! Downtown where newcomers come, where newcomers learn to become American with an accent!"

A Better Spring There Could Not Be

The winter of 1926-27 hurried by, or so it seemed. There were the usual difficulties associated with winter - confinement to quarters, difficult walks to the grocery stores and other businesses serving the neighborhood. As long as it seemed safe for Elna, she ventured out to take care of duties that belonged to the position of homemaker. Carl trudged through snow and ice often climbing mini-mountains created by the snow plows at each intersection as he went to work each weekday morning. Each of these activities was one that prolonged the winter a bit as it had done each year since their arrival in the U.S.A.

But much of the real winter of 1926-27 came in 1927 - interrupted from time to time - by springtime which tried to make its appearance. By early March, daffodils and crocuses on the south side of each home broke their way through the residual snow and other things which served as blankets for their deep winter of sleep. Immediately after New Year's came Harold's birthday - his first - and his vitality and desire for learning provided a good deal of entertainment.

Newfound friends for Elna begged for her attention with the thought that she could improve her tries at learning the English language - such as could be learned from those who were also curious about that new language. The men with whom Carl walked to work always had a new story or a grievance about the treatment of foreigners both in the neighborhood and the workplace. Some of the Danish people with whom Carl and Elna had become acquainted at *Vor Frelsers Kirke* and/or the Brotherhood's White Street Hall were neighborhood residents, and the new social life seemed to alleviate somewhat the strain of winter for them.

High on the agenda for attention was the forthcoming birth of a child to the Olsen household. Neighbor women were highly attentive during Elna's pregnancy and especially as the time for birth came closer. House visits from the physician assured Elna that things were going well. Carl, who had been somewhat oblivious to Elna's daily concerns about the event, was now also more attentive.

Springtime, the increasing attention from neighbors, fellow Danes and Carl, gave a sense of brevity to the winter, but the last week of March and the early weeks of April weighed heavily on Elna so that it seemed that winter had not really come to an end. But even that time hastened when Carl arrived home from work on April 21. The contractions which the doctor had talked about had started, and Carl was sent to the closest neighbor with a telephone to give report to the doctor who promised to be on hand. Mrs. Yedziniak appeared as she had promised and said that she would stay the night. "I'll use the couch," she said, "if I get sleepy." But Carl sent her home to sleep, promising to get her if she was needed. In the morning it was clear that she was needed, and Carl did as he promised. Just a few short steps for his long legs and he was at the home of Mrs. Yedziniak, who called the doctor and then headed immediately for the Olsen rental unit.

"It's a girl!" was the doctor's announcement as he, Mrs. Yedziniak and another close neighbor lady stood by to give assistance.

When calm had returned to the house, Elna asked if Carl would call Mrs. Back. Marie Back had been a nurse in Denmark and had indicated that she would help. She came as soon as she could after a walk of about fifteen blocks from where she and her husband, John Back, ran a dairy behind their home on Lincoln Street. When asked about John, she said, "Oh, he can take care of himself - and," as an afterthought, "the cat." Never at a loss for words, Marie Back chattered the entire time she spent with Elna on Grandview Terrace.

"Oh, she's such a beautiful baby!' she said of the new child whose name was to be Alice Catherine. Elna glowed! She had gotten the girl that she had wanted. Regularly she made it known that she was happy that she had gotten a boy first, but a girl the second time "couldn't have been better."

In a few days Carl, Elna and Harold could return to a routine, interrupted on a regular basis by the new person and voice and the specific responsibilities of a new mother.

With all of the excitement, the household had forgotten another important matter on the agenda through much of the winter. With an anticipated new member in the family, Carl and Elna had talked about a new place of residence. The new place, they said, should be closer to work, closer to church, closer to people who could visit from time to time - their own kind of people - Danes, that is.

Carl had been talking to the men with whom he walked and worked, learning from them about space in the apartments which were a block or two from work. He also asked about costs. From time to time Carl inquired where the rental signs appeared in the windows of the vacant units. Near the end of May - and Elna had had an opportunity to look at it in the latter part of May - they had found a very practical five-room flat on the second floor at 144 Putnam Street. Besides being much closer to work (about four blocks) the landlord had assured them that

58

they could rent out a room to help with the rent. "There's always somebody looking for a single room," the landlord said. It seemed too good to be true, but it was true, and on the first of June plans were in place to move the family of four to "one-forty-four."

As it turned out, there were very few of their own kind of people in the neighborhood, except to say that most of them were immigrants, willing to do the factory work of the major factories which bordered the neighborhood to the north and to the west. Hartford Steam Boiler was nearby, and next door to it was Hartford Machine Screw Company with Arrow, Hart and Heggeman across the street south of the boiler operation.

Up one block to the west and down a flight of 100 steps with a short walk across a bridge over the Park River ("Hog River" - as the neighbors called it) were Underwood Typewriter and Merrow Machine Company, the maker of high speed over-seam sewing machines.

A single block south from the front door of the apartment was a shopping center where everyone except Sears, Roebuck and G. Fox and Company maintained an adequate inventory of every conceivable need for blue collar families from all of Europe and the Mediterranean basin.

A bus stopped right outside the front door, if one could afford the fare (three tokens for one quarter). In one direction the bus traveled the mile and one-half to within walking distance of the Danish Brotherhood Hall on White Street. In the other direction it went to downtown Hartford - less than one mile away. *Vor Frelsers Kirke* was a long block north and a short block east from 144.

"What could have been more perfect?" said Elna, when she addressed her family and friends.

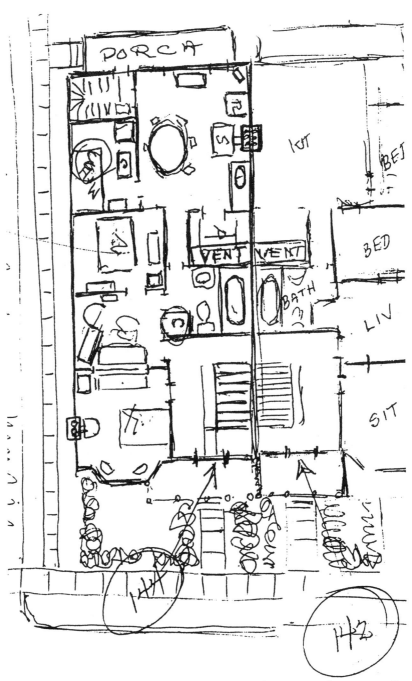

The floor plan of the "nice clean place" on the second
floor of one-forty-four

60

One-Forty-Four

One-Forty Four

One-forty-four was not a holy number. It was an address for three five-room flats of a six tenement house - a house built in the seventies of the 19th century. Evidence of its vintage were seen throughout the house. All water pipes (cold water only) were at the center of the structure - not behind plastered walls, but out in the open, since all water pipes were of lead and were subject to corrosion, leakage and repair and/or replacement. Each room had a gas jet for illumination, and in the kitchen, for the installation of a gas stove for cooking. Electricity was installed when it became available. A

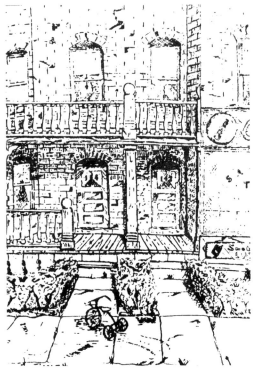

One-forty-four Putnam Street

chimney at the center of the structure and toward the back of the house vented coal stoves (space heaters). Two other chimneys were at the front of the house on the outside walls, lined with tile so that each level could have its own chimney. The front rooms were heated on a "sliding scale" - the room with the stove (coal heater) obviously warmer than the room that was to benefit from being nearby.

The flats were sometimes called "railroad flats" by virtue of the fact that rooms were one behind the other and when all doors were standing open the rooms appeared to be in the same succession as railroad cars were to each other. If one were sitting in the front room and needed something in the kitchen which was the most distant room to the rear, the trip needed to be a planned trip. The third room back was a bedroom, and if the occupant of that room was in bed, any passage through that room was an imposition on privacy. A small bathroom which flanked that room served as an alternate passage - it had both a

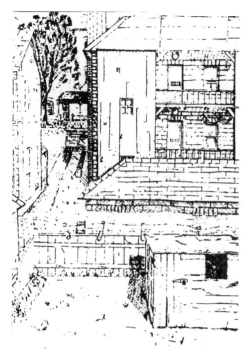

**Scene from the back porch
of one-forty-four**

front door and a back door - but often that room was sealed to provide the necessary privacy.

The bathrooms, described only briefly above, were at the center of the house by virtue of their being serviced by the water that flowed through the exposed pipe in every flat. In addition to the water service to the bathrooms, the bathrooms of all six tenements were serviced by a ventilation shaft which ran through the core of the house. Interesting sounds and often obnoxious odors flowed freely through that shaft to the outside.

"Behaeve yearseff, or I'll guive yea de baack of me hand" was one of the sounds, and it was often followed by a smack on the rear end by an "Aerish meether" who meant business in the Saturday night bathing program for the family. The smack was often followed by a wail of pain of the child just "hand printed" by his or her mother on "the you know where." On Saturday night, privacy was a "functional privacy" not a virtual reality and some very interesting things could be learned, if one wanted to learn them.

The front door of one-forty-four was never locked (fire regulations of tenement buildings which had more than two levels of occupancy demanded that such doors never be locked). Through that door passed the 25 to 30 people who lived in the three flats serviced by that door. Occasionally there was a visitor or two, who also entered by that door and on a regular basis, a drunk lay at the foot of the stairs by which second and third floor tenants gained access to their units. Beside the front door hung three mail boxes, each labeled with the name of a tenant family. Then, as now, the mailman delivered mail correctly, but substitute delivery people added interest, if not conflict, with the misdelivery of mail and other items.

But one-forty-four was only one-half of a building which had companion flats behind the number one-forty-two, companion flats only because there were three levels. Levels two and three were a "flip flop" version of the comparable levels at 144. The first floor of that side of the building was a divided flat with the front two rooms converted to "the neighborhood store". Room one at the front of that flat was the sales area and room two behind that served as the storage room for daily deliveries of the variety of items needed on a daily basis, or on a moment's notice by the two-hundred or so families whose normal route to larger shops on Park Street took them by this little "hole-in-the-wall" store.

The front entrances and their appended porches served as community centers where the languages of the neighborhood provided a kind of privacy to things that mattered to people who lived there - a neighborhood which consisted of only a fraction of the people who lived in an area of about 16,000 people of a variety of neighborhoods that constituted the place referred to as "Frog Hollow." The front entrances and their appended porches became community centers for people of all kinds of ethnic backgrounds who over time were to become Americans.

One-forty-four was the address that Elna and Carl had selected as a place suitable for a young Danish family who had chosen the city of Hartford as the place where they would live and raise a family in the new land across the seas from their sacred homeland, Denmark. It was the place about which Elna had made the comment, "What could be more perfect!"

What Could Be More Perfect?

When Elna had made her remark, "What could be more perfect!," little was she aware of the imperfections that were part of 144. For a young set of parents a daily trip down and up a flight of stairs was no difficulty at all - except when a drunk lay sprawled out at the foot of the common stairway to flats on the second and third floors. It did not happen often - on average maybe every week or two. Those who lay there were often those who dropped in their drunken stupor on the front deck of the "ma and pa" grocery story at the front of 142 and needed to be put somewhere out of sight. It was always startling, even when somewhat prepared, to find that one had to "strategize" one's way past a limp body, difficult enough when one was alone, but with two little children and perhaps a little bag of groceries, it became a challenge.

Dirt, common old ordinary dirt, plus the accumulation of debris from thoughtless people on the street, or even in the apartment building itself, called for a bit of cleaning every now and then. A quick review of the other residents in the building made it plain that the cleaning job would fall to Elna. Mary O'Malley, who lived on the third floor with three of her grown sons was physically incapable of cleaning the two flights of stairs with their intervening halls. Occasionally she would try on the flight of stairs that went to her flat, but Elna found herself cleaning all of it most of the time.

Water pipes banged with regularity, shaking the entire apartment structure. The phenomenon occurred when people in the house at 142 as well as at 144 suddenly turned the water off instead of gently closing the faucet. Where people had their own hot water heater, banging was especially common as steam, entrapped in the system, contributed to a regularly noisy water system.

The eleven Murphy children who lived with their parents on the first floor were usually considerate of the neighbors - though some of the older children who worked to support the family came in at very late hours. On work nights, Mary and Irene, came quietly. Edward, the third oldest, was not always so thoughtful. On party nights the hour was always late and lubrication from the nearest social hall, usually a tavern nearby, made for some noisy entrances due to unsteadiness of legs and feet. A good chorus from "When Irish Eyes Are Smiling" made it clear that it had been a glowing night with friends.

The Flannigan boys, sons of Mary O'Malley by her first marriage, made entrances into the building in their own and individually unique ways. Maury, the eldest, made his entrance with dispatch. The sound of rustling keys and quick steps on the stairway - indicating that he took two steps at a time - came and went as Maury hastily made his way to his room. Occasionally there was a flush of the toilet that could be heard everywhere. John, who was second and the best looking of the young men who lived on the third floor, took hours in ascending the two flights of stairs. With evidence of a long evening of socializing at a nearby pub, John entered the house in a near unconscious condition, often falling back down the stairs several times before being successful in his attempt at always being home before it was time to go to work the next morning. Ted, who was mentally retarded and not capable of regular employment, combed the common hallways in both the front and the back of the house - "just looking for the cat." Edward, who was the only O'Malley of the four boys, was still in eighth grade, and came and went as the school hours dictated. "He's a nice buy (Irish for "boy"). I believe he will finish high school!" Mrs. O'Malley would say. The other boys did not finish high school. When making reference to the three eldest, Mrs. O'Malley would say wistfully, "Their father was a good man." Where Eddy's father was concerned, there was complete silence.

But people were not the only things that were not perfect. Almost everything in the house was old. Water pipes broke on a regular basis or got plugged with rust or other debris in the water system. Electrical systems went "on the fritz" by virtue of their age or by virtue of a blown fuse, replaced by a trip to a dark and dingy basement electrical panel which was read regularly by a man from the Hartford Electric Light Company.

Leaks from poor soldering on an only slightly angled flat roof penetrated with regularity the third floor apartments, but often that water made it all the way through the building to the already damp basement. Leaks from overflowing sinks and bathtubs were a frequent occasion with a commensurate scream from someone in another flat that, "You left the water running in the sink, you dummy!" Odoriferous leaks from overflowing toilet bowls were not uncommon and the process of sanitizing everything in sight that looked wet made for many unpleasant tasks.

Monday was wash day! The stir of crank washing machines or newly purchased electrical ones (hand wringers, of course) were in evidence for most of the morning on that day of the week. Trash hauling by horse-drawn garbage wagons (extra long) made for a symphony of sounds from a variety of trash barrels (wooden to fancy steel ones) down in the alley behind the house. Street vendors, riding their horse-drawn vehicles, called out their very familiar refrains so that busy wives and mothers could take advantage of the goods and services they provided, or did not provide (usually on the day of greatest need).

Most piercing of all of the sounds were those that sounded on a Sunday morning when someone had stolen the roast that was being planned for the Sunday meal. Electrical refrigeration was a known possibility, but no one at 144 was fortunate enough to have it. All refrigeration, if it could be called that, was by ice boxes cooled with blocks of ice, from the ice man. The ice boxes occupied the landing space just outside the door of the flat in the back hall of the house. The hunger which plagued the inner city - even in the prosperous twenties, made theft from ice boxes a fairly common occurrence.

With all of these risks and inconveniences at 144, there were still many benefits which enabled Elna to say, "What could be more perfect!"

The "More Perfect" Place

"One-forty-four" couldn't have been more perfect in many ways, inspite of the imperfections of a building which was showing its more than fifty years of wear and one which housed families with all kinds of lifestyles and habits that tested the most stalwart of residents.

Two things loomed large for Elna as she made her assessment of the new place in which she and Carl and the children were going to live. The first of these was the proximity of that address to Carl's place of employment. Now, instead of the twenty-two-block walks to and from work, the walks were only five minutes which represented a saving of one to two hours each day, depending largely on the season of the year.

The extra hours were precious to Elna who had found the days at one-hundred-and-twenty-seven Grandview Terrace to be very long on many occasions. Though surrounded by many people, kindred spirits were hard to come by in the multi-ethnic and multi-cultural neighborhood in which she lived. Even with a growing command of the language, the constant meeting of the vast variety of life expressions, was not conducive to developing deep and lasting relationships. Her need for Carl as companion was a great need on occasion and the extra hours going to and from work stole time from those important encounters. In addition to sharing their common heritage, Elna enjoyed hearing of Carl's contact with the new world. Coupled with her own limited exposure, the daily news from Carl provided a growing opportunity for "accommodation," if not "assimilation," into the new world.

The second thing which loomed large for Elna in declaring one-forty-four as "more perfect" was the proximity to Our Savior's Danish Lutheran Church. The weekly worship gathered Danes from all over central Connecticut, it seemed, and Elna looked forward to every opportunity for worship which included an opportunity to share a cherished Danish heritage where every custom and every kind of food did not need an explanation. Andersens, Pedersens, Christensens, Begtrups, Hostrups, Kirkegaards and Ostergaards - those who gathered - were a cross section of everything Danish that was deep in Elna's soul. To meet with them on a regular basis was to experience renewal and to gather strength for the challenges of the days between Sundays.

The fact that the parsonage was adjacent to the church added an extra benefit. On very nice days it was refreshing to walk the one and one-half blocks to the parsonage for a little visit with the Pastor Henning-Lund Sorensen family. She knew he was a busy man, but she also knew that on most occasions he enjoyed putting down his duties for a little visit with Elna and her two children, for he, too, longed for the familiar Danish tongue and the treasures that could be shared from memories of Denmark.

When it happened that the pastor and his family were not at home, the baby park which was on the way to the pastor's home was available for a short swing or a brief look at nature. The baby park was a pocket-sized park in the middle of the factory and residential district where Carl and Elna lived. In addition to the swings, it provided public bath facilities, two tennis courts, horse-shoe pits and a place to feed pigeons which cooed and strutted for whatever attention they could get. Elna always planned to have a handful of popped corn to keep both the pigeons and the children entertained.

If the only two assets that were available to Elna were that of shortened work hours for Carl and the proximity of their address to the Danish Church, it would have been enough. But one-forty-four was less than a mile from the heart of Hartford where all of the major department stores of the day displayed their wares in artistic elegance. G. Fox & Co (the nearest thing to Marshall Fields of Chicago), located on Main Street was the main department store for central Connecticut. Next to Fox's was Sage Allen and Browne-Thompson's, both fashion stores with the latest to show. Sears, Roebuck & Co. was just a block south and around the corner. Across the street from Sears was the transfer island of the Connecticut Bus Company, where one could board a bus to most places within twenty miles of Hartford. In the other direction on Main Street from Fox's was Marholen's - Hartford's leading hardware store together with the predecessors to the fast food industry, including a White Castle Hamburger Restaurant.

A side benefit to the journey to Hartford's center was the fact that only four blocks from home was the spacious and well kept grounds of the Connecticut State Capitol Building from which one could view the stately Horace Bushnell Memorial Auditorium (the home of the Hartford Symphony and the traveling New York Theater Companies). Next to the auditorium was the home of the Hartford Insurance Company with its two magnificent cast-iron lions - each on a pedestal flanking a broad but gradual stairway to the main entrance of the building.

The trip to town was a nice afternoon's outing, even with the children in tow. If the journey ended at the state capitol grounds, it could hardly be considered a disappointment. Hartford, the park city, was at its most beautiful on those grounds within just blocks of one-forty-four.

Here was a city, beautiful to enjoy and with the best of retail shopping just minutes away! Was there anything else that could make it "more perfect?" Yes, and Elna would discover it, during the more than thirty-five years that she lived on the second floor of one-forty-four.

Park Street

Just as important, if not more so, than the city center "with the best of everything," was Park Street. On Park Street, which was just one and one-half blocks south of one-forty-four, you could find everything you needed, and often at a discount.

Spain's Department Store, commonly known only as Spain's, sold everything in clothing and cloth - almost always at a discount ("Seconds" Mary O'Malley used to say to Elna). If customers showed any hesitation about buying the underwear they were looking at, Mr. Spain was there in what seemed like a second to offer a pair of socks "free" with the purchase, thereby enhancing the discount. "This is real quality, Mrs. Olsen," he would say, as he laid out the socks for inspection. Mr. Spain usually made the sale.

Dominick F. Burns owned and operated a "super" meat market, which carried almost everything in groceries that went with meat (fish on Wednesdays and Fridays). Mr. Burns, whose business was a thriving business, made it a point of knowing his customers by name. He also knew much of their household circumstances and often offered a helping hand by providing his products at "a price especially for you, Mrs. Hagen." Occasionally a customer got a "bone for the dog" after which he whispered, "It will make good soup, you know."

On the way to Burn's "super market" was Louie Bloom's Fresh Produce, products which were delivered by the middlemen, who met the produce ships docked at the foot of State Street on the Connecticut River. From as far away as Argentina and the New York ports on the New Jersey side of the Hudson River, the ships carried everything in the vegetable and fruit line to round out an otherwise bland meal of meat and/or fish and potatoes - accompanied by "day old bread" from the Bond Baking Company, a few blocks off Park Street.

On the corner of Park and Broad Streets was a bank which stayed open until 9:00 p.m. on payday, always a Friday and until noon on Saturday. There were no checks to cash as everyone was paid in cash, but savings accounts abounded with nickel and dime deposits "for the rainy day." There were very few, if any, college-bound young people among the immigrants who considered completion of high school as a major achievement. Young people were expected to work at age sixteen. Often they lied about their age and started at fourteen to help support the family, a duty from which they were released at age eighteen when they were expected to be "out of the nest" and "taking care of themselves." They were also savers.

71

Kazarian's, a shoe repair shop which also "blocked" felt hats, worked overtime with all of the members of the family providing some part of the service being performed. Almost all families expected shoes to last through three restorations - inspite of the fact that new Tom McAnn shoes for men could be purchased for a little over $6.00 a pair. David, the eldest boy, was as proficient as his father and was expected to follow in his father's "shoes." But when it became clear that David had an above average intelligence, together with a zeal for learning, the shoe repair mantle passed on to a younger boy, Leonard, with David going on to college "to learn how to be an accountant."

Park Street, for approximately seven blocks west of Hungerford Street to Zion Street also boasted fourteen taverns where both men and women gathered for socialization and refreshment. "Ballentines" was the beer of choice in most of the taverns. Each tavern was noted as much for its atmosphere as it was for its beverages, and regulars were a part of the scene every night. Of the fourteen taverns, several were known for providing "special services" from the ladies who occupied certain apartments above the establishments. As closing time approached each evening - usually at 11:00 p.m. - limp bodies were tossed to the sidewalks to "sober up" enough to make the journey home to one of the many flats that surrounded Park Street. The flats all together housed from 18,000 to 20,000 people in the 30 square block area known as "Frog Hollow."

But not all was commerce and conviviality. Seventeen churches could be found in Frog Hollow, some reflecting ethnic groups that were no longer dominant in the neighborhood with others clearly serving the residents currently occupying the decaying community. The dominant churches in the late twenties of the twentieth century were Roman Catholic (Immaculate Conception for the Irish and St. Ann's for the French - Canadian.) Both churches were open around the clock with votive candles providing a haunting atmosphere of God's presence on earth. Next in prominence was Immanuel Lutheran Church (Swedish) on the corner of Capitol Avenue and Broad Street with St. George's Eastern Orthodox (Greek) Church in the middle of the first block on Broad Street south from Immanuel Lutheran. Most of the other churches served non-resident communities - communities that had been well represented in the area at the turn of the century. Grace Lutheran (German) and Our Savior's Lutheran (Danish) stood diagonally across from each other at the intersection of Russ and Babcock Streets with only a few of their members still in the community.

For a small pocket of Swedes who were still in the neighborhood around Hungerford and Russ Streets there was a Mission Covenant Church with a faithful but dwindling membership

During the week the language of the street was broken English as workers, mostly men, journeyed to and from their factory jobs. On the weekends when the nearby factories operated with only a skeleton crew the language was mostly Irish at the east end of Frog Hollow and French-Canadian at the west end of the neighborhood. If one was a Protestant living in the neighborhood, it was almost like swimming upstream against the majority cultures.

Park Street and Frog Hollow became very much a part of life for Carl and Elna and their children, but Sunday was an especially welcomed day for Carl and Elna together with Harold and Alice. Sunday provided refreshment for their souls, both spiritually and culturally, and life took on a glow that lasted from week to week in their newfound land and in the community in which they lived. In the last analysis, it was really Our Savior's Lutheran Church that was the most important ingredient of their days at 144.

Vor Frelsers Kirke

Our Savior's Evangelical Lutheran Church, founded on May 31, 1891, outlived its founders, many of whom lived only a few years in the neighborhood in which the church was built. Like many new congregations, Our Savior's began in the homes of its early members with pastors - mostly from New York - serving periodically to administer the sacraments and "give a real sermon." As the church grew, it was determined that a church building should be built.

A committee, appointed to the task, recommended that a lot on the corner of Russ and Babcock Streets be purchased for a proposed church and that the lot next door be purchased for a future parsonage. By the end of the year, 1893, a handsome church was built in European and Danish tradition. A basement, which was not in European and/or Danish tradition, was to serve as the foundation for the building which was to rise from that base high into the sky. There was little thought of Sunday School space in the planning, but the basement which could be entered from street level could provide for storage of liturgical items, for heating facilities and for toilets for both men and women. Since tenement living did not provide enough space to gather the Danes socially, it was thought that the basement could also serve as a social hall for meetings of one kind or another - mostly lectures and other edifying presentations.

The church, itself, was a frame structure with brick veneer and a gabled roof above which the steeple would rise another twenty feet for all in the neighborhood to see. Twenty steps, with a landing at the thirteenth step, rose to the front door where a narthex, flanked by two closets for winter wear, gave opportunity for a brief greeting by the president of the congregation upon entrance and a farewell blessing from the pastor upon departure. The center aisle, covered with a burgundy carpet, led to the chancel area, three steps above the sanctuary floor. To the right of the chancel was a sacristy from which the pastor could enter an elevated pulpit to proclaim God's word to His people. To the left was a small landing where numbers for the hymnboard were stored and access to the basement could be gained.

A three-paneled reredos rose above the altar with a cross topping each panel. In the center panel the Resurrection was proclaimed by a painting with an angel in white presenting the empty tomb. An altar rail with cushioned kneeler surrounded an area from which the pastor could distribute the communion elements. Opposite the pulpit stood the baptismal font with a cross-topped lid - carefully crafted by one of the members.

At the rear of the church was a balcony with "the best organ that money could buy" and with space for a choir consisting mostly of children of Sunday School age.

In each of six arched windows on either side of the sanctuary stained glass windows told the story of the faith that was to be proclaimed there on Sundays and on special festivals of the Church Year such as Christmas, Easter and Pentecost.

V.A.M. Mortensen was called from Denmark to be the first pastor. Arriving in 1894, he served the congregation until 1901. Pastor Mortensen was the first of seven pastors who served the congregation, before the arrival from Denmark of Pastor Henning Lund-Sorensen who was the pastor when Carl and Elna and their children arrived in the Frog Hollow neighborhood. Among the seven who served before the 1927 arrival of the Olsen family were two well known Danish-American pastors, namely Svend Marckmann and Svend Jorgensen, who were more Danish than American in some ways, but very capable men for the newly established Our Savior's Lutheran Church.

Initially for the Olsens, Our Savior's Lutheran Church was Pastor Lund-Sorensen and a very beautiful worship facility. But as time went by in Carl and Elna's residency Our Savior's Lutheran Church became people, worshipping people, who took their place regularly in the pews raising their voice in song and listening with dedication to the pastor's message.

Down in front on the right hand side under the pulpit sat Peter Mose - a man of great faith and a powerful voice that proclaimed that faith in song. Peter often walked to church - a distance of about twenty blocks. On inclement days, in the winter in particular, he rode a Connecticut Company bus to the corner of Capital Avenue and Babcock Streets from which he walked one block to the church. He sat directly under the pulpit, sometimes in bowed position and sometimes with his head leaned far backward so that he could see the pastor as well as hear him. Across the sanctuary in the third pew back from the baptismal font sat Bianco and Christine Brylle (Christine was the daughter of a charter member family) with one or more of their children

Midway on the baptismal side sat Aksel and Carrie Christensen Krogh together with Janet, their daughter, and Paul, their son. Again, on the other side of the church sat Jens Bossen - a grocer in Windsor, Connecticut, and a widower - with his daughter, Elizabeth. They regularly sat in the sixth pew back from the pulpit and on the aisle. The Bossens usually came by auto from Windsor, several miles north of Hartford on the Connecticut River. From West Hartford came the Thomsens with their daughter, Inger. By car came Oscar and Marian Piper from Newington. Most of those who came in the mid to late twenties lived some distance from the church.

It was a full church when Carl and Elna and the children came the first time. Not infrequently thereafter Carl and Elna came early to help the elderly make the last of the twenty steps into the church and to help them again as they descended the stairs for their labored walks to their homes nearby or to Connecticut Company buses that would take them to the towns surrounding the city of Hartford.

Such a joy it was to sing the familiar hymns and songs. "*I Østen stiger solen op*" was always a favorite. The sun did shine in all of its splendor into Elna's kitchen at one-forty-four almost every day. And as it did, it brought a little bit of Sunday into the house each day. "*Gud, du bevarer os vel!*" she would say and, indeed, God did care for them well, she thought.

The Holidays in 1927

With the birth of Alice in April and a move in mid-summer, the year 1927 seemed to vanish. Suddenly it was November! What had happened to July, August, September and October? They just disappeared into the excitement of life. A new child. A new residence with more space than the young Olsen couple had experienced since their marriage in November of 1924. A new neighborhood. And most importantly, Our Savior's Lutheran Church - a place for and of renewal, a place where the language of the heart prevailed, both culturally and spiritually, providing nourishment for the Danish soul that lived within Elna. "I pinch myself every now and then about how good we have it," she would say often over the next many months.

With rhythmic regularity the days sped by, and then there was a new experience for Carl and Elna and their children. It was called "Thanksgiving." About ten days before the day of celebration, store windows on Park Street began displaying turkeys (not real ones) with fanned tails strutting in a field of Connecticut grown cornstalks and wheat. Beside them stood a figure of a Pilgrim with his buckled high hat and belt, musket in hand, telling the story of early America with its hardships of winter and its cornucopia of agricultural abundance which was to see them through those hardships and on into the new year.

There were few parallels for this Danish couple and other immigrants three-hundred years after the first Thanksgiving had been celebrated. The decorations said, "Doesn't everyone celebrate Thanksgiving?" "Doesn't everyone have turkey for this day of honored remembrance in American history?" The answer was clearly, "No." It was a new holiday with which the new immigrants were to become acquainted, with foods that did not appear in foreign cookbooks and stories about a past that were clearly important to immigrants who had come mostly from England in the early seventeenth century.

A brief visit into the hearts and souls of the new immigrants to Frog Hollow would have made it clear that this celebration was a foreign holiday - a holiday with which they needed to become familiar.

The first Thanksgiving at 144 was not a celebration in the American tradition, but it was a celebration of settlement for the new pilgrims, in this case from Denmark. The special food was not turkey, but pork. *Flæskesteg* - a pork roast (with prunes) - that was not on the menu every day. Such a "center of the plate" treat was reserved for special occasions and so this first Thanksgiving at 144 was. Carrots, peas, red cabbage, homemade bread and potatoes with beautiful brown gravy rounded out the menu to make this a very special meal for a very special moment in life. Would that it could have been celebrated with family! But such was not to be the case. Nor did it become an occasion for joining with friends, most of whom were still to be gathered in the days that lay ahead.

Thanksgiving evening was spent in letter writing - mostly to Denmark. *Bedstemor* and *Bedstefar* as they were being designated after the birth of two grandchildren were at the head of the list. But there were notes to send to members of the family who followed Elna and Christine to America, beginning with one to Christine who did not move on to Connecticut as Carl and Elna had done. Three other siblings who had emigrated to America were also on the list for letters, together with notes to *Moster* Karen (*Bestemor's* sister) and Uncle Rudolf and Uncle Peter (*Bestemor's* brother) and *Tante* Marie, both of whom - by coincidence, Danish coincidence - were Hansen families.

The Thanksgiving Day weekend passed quietly, with Carl leaving the scene at home from time to time to tend to the banked furnaces and to make sure everything was in order for the new week to begin when the scene and sounds of Putnam Street and vicinity returned to the usual patterns of latter day pilgrims who were gaining a new life in the industrial and entrepreneurial East - in this case, Hartford.

It was only days after Thanksgiving that the Advent Season began, the season preparatory to Christmas. With the arrival of Advent, the pace increased on Park and Putnam Streets, but it was not the merchants who created the new pace nor benefitted a great deal from it. The pace had to do with the religious obligations of good Catholic Christians, who had extra devotional exercises with which to be concerned. Wednesdays and Fridays took on the significance of fast days. Menus for the stomach changed, but so did menus for spiritual preparation for the holy days ahead.

While the men were expected to carry on pretty much as they would at any other time in providing for the family, the women and children were obviously in a different mode. Long lines of parochial school children were formed in the school yards next to the churches with the sisters of their particular school responsible for disciplining those who stepped out of line. Each grade in its turn was directed to the church for Mass and such prayers as would prepare their souls for the arrival of the Christ child. If one lived anywhere near the intersection of Park and Putnam Streets, one had to notice the activity. All day long the priests and the sisters of St. Anne's Church (French) with their children paraded in and out of the rather majestic structure built to the Glory of God in honor of St. Anne.

What was true at Park and Putnam Streets was also true at Park and Hungerford Streets where Immaculate Conception Church (Irish) also had a parochial school with grades one through eight. Their uniform dress was different from that of the St. Anne's children, but the religious exercise was the same. The same was true for the parish of Sts. Cyril and Methodius (Lithuanian) Church on Broad Street and Capitol Avenue.

The three Roman Catholic churches in Frog Hollow set the tone for living through the seasons of the year and not unmeaningfully, the Church's liturgical year. Occasionally the Eastern Orthodox Church on Broad Street yielded its influence, too, but their time table was different as was their expression for the various liturgical holidays.

Most Protestant Churches gave no evidence of their participation in Advent preparations except on the hymn-board at the front of the sanctuary where the name at the top said, "ADVENT ONE," "ADVENT TWO" and so on up until Christmas Eve. What the Roman Catholics did gave greater significance to what Lutherans did - even Danish Lutherans. And occasionally Danish Lutherans even took note of the Greek festivals associated with St. George's Orthodox Church, noting that Christmas was celebrated on Epiphany Day in that tradition.

As the season progressed it became clear that some of the activity on Park Street was related to Christmas shopping. Special merchandise and special foods were placed in prominence for the church goers and others to notice as possible fare for the holidays. Business was very clearly brisk as the Christmas holidays drew closer and the last minute shopper was very much in evidence. Tempers which were to be tempered with love clearly grew shorter, and store clerks served with diminished patience. But each business benefitted from the holiday celebrated in the community.

Elna now found herself part of that scene. With her two children she made her way to Park Street every now and then, not only to shop for the necessities, but - in this season - to discover bargains that could be purchased as gifts for the household for Christmas and for the needy children at the church. Elna did not personally know anyone who was poor, but she was sure that there were some in that circumstance, and conversations with Pastor Henning Lund-Sorensen confirmed her suspicions.

Sometimes Elna returned from Park Street empty handed. Her money did not reach, and sometimes there was no money at all, but it was a good outing to see how people lived in America. Occasionally, too, she met a neighbor with whom she had already gotten acquainted from whom she could gain information about how to function in the pluralistic culture in which she now found herself thoroughly immersed. She also got to know the merchants who sometimes stood outside their establishments. But, maybe more important, those merchants got to know who Mrs. Olsen on Putnam Street was. Both the neighbor and the merchant relationships were part of her strategy to make the best of things that already seemed pretty good to her.

The pluralism of the neighborhood was interesting and challenging, but every now and then it was important for Elna to keep and strengthen her ties with Danes.

The most important contact with the Danes was Our Savior's Danish Lutheran Church, and on the major holidays - Easter, Christmas and Pentecost - Danes came from everywhere in the state of Connecticut; some as far away as Boston in the neighboring state to the north, too. Their occupations and/or titles were as varied as life itself: fishermen and farmers, dairymen, tool and die makers, grocers, tailors, auto salesmen, cement workers and tradesmen, boarding house keepers and beauticians, Watkins Product distributors, streetcar conductors, librarians and artists, curators and railroad conductors - all were among the collection of Danes who found the church at the center of their lives on the major Christian holidays.

"You never know, ven you may needt the Pastor. It is always good to know who he iss," was often heard. "You couldt vant to get married, you know!" the single men said. "Yah, andt kitzener needt to get baptized, too" could be heard from across the room. There was usually some kind of a social gathering associated with the major church holidays. All were expressions of the Danish Lutheran Church as it came to be in America.

A second important contact with Danes was at the "White Street Hall," the home of The Danish Brotherhood and The Danish Sisterhood. The activity was clearly social - liquid refreshments were almost always a part of the mix with dancing to the liveliest of Danish dance music also part of the scene. Occasionally there would be a visit from someone from the Danish Embassy in New York or the local Danish Consulate where the new American-Danes could find help with a variety of immigration problems, as well as family difficulties in Denmark that needed special attention from people with special privilege and authority.

80

In a very real sense the Danish Church and the Danish Brotherhood were twin hearts for Danes in America and each was sought out for its particular emphasis. Elna's greatest loyalty was to Our Savior's Lutheran Church for at least a couple of reasons beginning with the proximity of 144 Putnam Street to the Church on Russ and Babcock Steets. A strong Grundtvigian exposure from the Danish Folk School movement also contributed to that commitment. Renewal was the essence of the Grundtvigian thrust in Denmark. It was logical that that should come to play also in America when Danish renewal was being sought by one steeped in the tradition.

Clearly the sacred and the secular played an important part in the preparations for the Christmas holidays, both in the neighborhood and in the inheritance of Denmark that immigrants brought with them to a land that was to be their home for the remainder of their lives.

The celebration of Christmas, though much influenced by the present circumstance of living in Frog Hollow and the twin heartbeat of things Danish in the Hartford area, found intimate expression in the home at 144.

Preparations had been going on at various times throughout the year - even before the move to 144, but certainly after the move. As the boxes were unpacked things were discovered that could be used for decoration of the five-room flat on the second floor. A piece of ribbon or a piece of string could be used in decorating a tree or wrapping a package. A piece of brown paper, if it was big enough, could be used to wrap a package for the family in Denmark. Set aside at the time of unpacking were pictures taken with the Brownie Camera - pictures which now were of two beautiful children - pictures which needed to be duplicated to be included in the next letter to Denmark.

About ten days before Christmas Carl was sent to Park Street to pick out a tree (before they all got picked over) that would fit their new quarters. A few candles for the tree - the kind that flicker - were set aside to use for only a few minutes so as to give a vital atmosphere to the celebration at home. After a brief moment of glow, the candles were extinguished, and the single strand of lights was turned on for a few brief hours each evening - not before, but after, Christmas Day. Christmas in the Danish tradition did not begin until church time on Christmas Eve and lasted until Holy Three Kings Day (Epiphany, January 6) at which time the tree was stripped of its ornaments and cut up to be collected at the curbside on the next garbage pickup day. Christmas gifts appeared mysteriously through the night , ready to be discovered under the tree on Christmas morning.

81

Throughout the morning hours of Christmas Day the aromas of a Danish Christmas wafted throughout the house. The smell of a cooking goose permeated all the other smells and the salivating associated with holiday feasting began. Even the red cabbage had to give way to the cooking goose. Rice pudding, which had been prepared the day before, gave off no aroma, but it did give off the promise of a special gift for the one who discovered an almond hidden in the pudding.

If the celebration of Christmas at home had an intimacy about it, the intimacy was enhanced with worship at Our Savior's Danish Lutheran Church. The Christmas Eve service was set for seven o'clock so that factory workers and all could get there and be on time. A Christmas tree with all white lights stood opposite the pulpit. At the top of the tree was a Christmas angel with its spun glass attire - giving it an ethereal quality. The hymnboard provided the numbers of Christmas favorites, all of which were sung with feeling and power.

"Det var midt i Julenat!" "Christmas is here with joy untold!" *"Et barn er født i Bethlehem!"* "The happy Christmas comes once more, The heavenly guest is at the door!"

The music, the words, the atmosphere, everything that said "Christmas" brought tears to the eyes and joy to the hearts of these people who were so far from their families and yet so near them all in their faith in God and His promises.

The sermon focused on God's gift, and Pastor Henning Lund-Sorensen was at his best with his scattered flock now gathered to hear God's Word of Love which came down at Christmas.

Thi eder er i dag en frelser født i Davids by; han er Kristus, Herren! Og dette skal være jer et tegn: I skal finde et barn svøbt og liggende i en krybbe.
Ære være Gud i det højeste! Og paa jorden fred i mennesker, der har hans velbehag!*

The words were in Danish. The words were of God. The words of the pastor affirmed the importance of those words to the Danes in America in the same way that they had been affirmed to those same people in years past in Denmark.

Until now Christmas had never been so important and so festive in America, but in the year 1927 Christmas became the vital moment of the year. And once again in the heart of Elna, she could hear her own words: "What could be more perfect?"

*This day a Savior is born in the city of David; he is Christ, the Lord! And this shall be a sign to you: You will find him in swaddling clothes and lying in a manger.

Glory be to God in the Highest! And on earth peace among men with whom he is well pleased!

Luke 2:11-12; 14

Zooming in on the 144 Neighborhood

A warm glow remained in Elna's heart as she reviewed the Christmas just past. Settled, at last! And with everything close at hand - not least Our Savior's Danish Lutheran Church, where Carl, Elna, Harold and Alice had just participated in a very special part of the social and worship life of that community. "Nu har vi Jul igen!" remained with her well into the new year of 1928.

Elna had said the Apostles' Creed many times, but never before had the phrase "the communion of saints" been as vivid for her as it had been in the Christmas celebration of the calendar year that had just now closed. For the first time since she and Carl had left the Perth Amboy, New Jersey, community of young Danes, Elna felt very strongly again that she was a part of a community with which she had something very important in common. Not all who belonged to that Danish community were saints in the common understanding of that word, but they were part of the faith community which confessed a common faith in God with a common understanding of life, and all of that felt very good to Elna.

By the time Christmas had arrived it appeared that Carl was secure in his job. It also appeared that the family could count on being in the new neighborhood and near to the Danish Lutheran Church for a long time. That, too, had added something to the contentment that was Elna's.

But, alas, there was the new neighborhood to discover - not the neighborhood that certainly was strategically located in the city of Hartford - but the neighborhood that consisted of the people who were the immediate neighbors. Like the church family her immediate neighbors were also to become a community for Elna.

Not always do those who live in closest proximity to one's place of residence become important in one's support community, but it became the case in this instance with Mr. Ludins, who was the landlord of the six-tenement apartment house at 142 and 144 Putnam Street. As it turned out, Mr. Ludins shared the other second floor of the building. Back porches, separated by only eighteen inches or so, provided a regular opportunity for visiting. On the last day of each month the encounter was especially significant as rent money exchanged hands for the next month, but so were days when Elna could provide a kind of support to the Ludins household, who as it turned out had needs that rent money could not cover.

84

In their quite frequent visits Elna soon learned that Mr. Ludins was a Jew by birth and religious persuasion. She also learned that Mr. Ludins - he had a first name, but none of the tenants ever used it - was a widower with a crippled daughter in her late twenties. Jenny was very young when she had the accident which left her almost completely paralyzed from her waist and down. She had fallen backwards from a ground floor porch or deck. As she fell her feet were caught in the porch railing, a fact which probably spared her from death. But the fall destined her for a lifetime on crutches. To make matters worse her mother died as she entered her teen years. Ludins, as he usually was called, knew he had to do something very different from what he was doing for a living when his wife died, and as he pondered what that should be, he concluded that apartment ownership would make it possible for him to be at home to assist his daughter. And so it did, and between the two of them they managed quite well. But Elna clearly could be helpful from time to time to Jenny who was nearly her same age.

There were regulars in the neighborhood who walked by on their way to work who Elna met - especially those whose work hours were later than the factory positions which demanded presence at the work place by 7:00 a.m. Among those who walked by was Mary Eagan who "wiggled" her way to work in shoes that looked like they hurt. Mary was employed by the Aetna Life Insurance Company Home Office on Farmington Avenue. Harry O'Toole also worked at Aetna, but held a position that allowed him to own a car. Harry drove to work, usually ten minutes after Mary passed 144. A private person, Harry was not given to greetings early in the morning, but he did learn to nod with a smile at Mrs. Olsen and her two children who occasionally were on the street as early as 8:00 a.m. Harry's sister, Marian, worked at the bank at the corner of Park and Affleck Streets and left about thirty minutes later than Harry. With names like Eagan and O'Toole one did not have to guess about religious affiliation.

Up the street (south one black) was an Italian family headed by Rocco Forte. Rocco was a painter by trade and did not follow a regular routine of coming and going. The two older children, Mary and Art, worked at Underwood Typewriter and Royal Typewriter respectively and were out of sight before Elna ventured onto the street. They followed the regular factory hours. Albert, the youngest, was still in grammar school. Speaking no English, Mrs. Forte was seldom seen on the street where she could exchange anything with the neighbors.

The Balickis were Polish and occupied the second floor of a well kept three story residence. Elna stopped to visit with Mrs. Balicki when, like Elna, she was out with her two children, Francis and Eddie, on a grocery errand or just on a walk to enjoy the weather when spring and fall put on their displays.

There were always people on the street, but not many were Danes, though there were a few. Just up the street on Mortson Street - in a third floor apartment, lived Helga Petersen with a "near-grown" son (he was eight) and a daughter who was almost three. Helga was a welfare mother who received assistance from the government by virtue of having been abandoned by her husband. Warren was in third grade with Louise not yet ready for kindergarten. Work for Helga did not seem readily available, nor did she particularly desire a job under the circumstances.

A Mrs. Larsen, Gudrun by name, lived on Grand Street and ran a boarding house - a "meals only" operation. With only a block to the grocery store from where she lived, she could venture away from her family to do the shopping required to make a living serving meals to single Danish men who either lived in the neighborhood or worked in the nearby factories or both.

A bit further away was Mrs. Marie Back, whose husband John, together with a brother whose name was Fred, maintained a milk operation including the pasteurization of raw milk brought to the city by dairy farmers who farmed small acreages adjacent to the city. A barn in the backyard behind the house on Lincoln Street housed an old horse, a milk wagon, and pasteurization equipment. Childless, Marie Back was free to make an occasional trip to Putnam Street to visit the "new" family. She became especially fond of Alice and often issued an invitation to Elna and her children to come over to "talk" to her cats - all "good mousers" - helpful around the dairy operation "out in the back."

With the passage of time Elna learned to know the O'Rourkes, the Evashevskis, the Formicas, the Foleys, the Sheas, the Goodnos, the Morottos, the Martocchios and the Mascones, the Kiczuks, the Gundelacks, the Pelletiers the Gervascios, the Cressottis and the Cwiklas - families that Elna chanced to meet on days that were nice enough to walk her children to Park Street, the "Baby Park," or an occasional visit to Pastor Lund-Sorensen's. Elna was soon to discover that her new neighborhood was a miniature Europe with people from all over that continent from which she had come and from the Mediterranean basin, which supplied new people for all parts of the world.

86

A Leap Year

The Christmas of 1927 lingered into 1928 as it should. The liturgical year of the Christian Church, which served as Elna's internal calendar, made it clear that Christmas of any year lasted until the day of the Epiphany, or Holy Three Kings Day, as Elna knew it. Included in that time - early in 1928 - was Harold's second birthday. The Christmas tree was always up for Harold's Birthday helping to retain the spirit of Christmas and on to Epiphany if the tree had not dried out too much. The time was festive.

When the holidays had passed, quiet set in. With the children in bed, or soon to be there, evenings often became long. Occupying the long evenings were letters written to members of the family, especially those in Denmark. On one such occasion Elna wrote to her sister, Dagmar - whose wedding day was soon to be held. Elna added such comments as came to her mind as she wrote for the occasion:

> I hope it goes well for you. It is good that he (Lago) will receive a stipend as he starts out on his life's work, because without help, I think it would be impossible to set up a home in Denmark. But when you have a little help and a bit of luck on your side, then there is no place better for us Danes than in beautiful Denmark, but then home is probably always the best place to be. Our nation is important, but the economy plays an important role - sometimes more important than it should, I think. Well, Carl has written a long letter to Lago. At the moment I am not motivated to write, so Carl will have to speak for the two of us. Now I must go to take "care" of Alice. She has to go to bed. We have been out until seven o'clock with the children. This is the first time that we have been out that late with the children, so Alice is so tired, so tired. Harold managed very well. Karna was here for a little while this evening with a little girl, so we took her home and Carl needed to go to work for a while to see that everything is working the way it should. He goes twice on holidays; there is always something for him to do. But we have it so good. Just so that it is always that way, then we will be without need, but we do not know what each day will bring and it is probably well that we do not know everything in advance. Hope you will write to us about a date for your wedding and how everything is going. Now I have to stop. I'm getting sleepy.
>
> Greet everyone there at home. Hope you are well. I will soon need to write Mom a thank you note for the Birthday letter that she sent to Harold.

Loving greetings from all four of us. Elna

I'm wondering if Mom got the two dollars from us for the 25th of October?

This letter, which was one of several written from time to time was a special letter prompted by the forthcoming wedding. Regular letters were written every Friday to *Bedstemor* (Elna's mother) that shared much of Elna's daily life in America. Now that both Harold and Alice made up a good part of her life, she shared much about the progress of the first of the grandchildren for her mother. Together with the letter went pictures, made possible by a newfound prosperity in the new country.

The pictures often revealed that the prosperity was modest - though adequate enough for the purchase of an automobile for occasional outings or visits to friends - most of whom did not live "close in" in the Hartford area. As the weather got warmer there were trips *"langt ud i skoven"* (to wooded park areas - scattered throughout central Connecticut not far from Hartford's city center).

Trips to Park Street were fairly frequent (even in the early days of the year) when the weather was nice, but rarely did such trips take place at night during the long and lonesome periods of the new life in the new neighborhood.

Visits from Karna, Elna's third sister, who had come to America in the early fall of 1926, were not as frequent as were the trips to Park Street, but her visits did from time to time alleviate the days of quiet that followed in regular progression throughout the year 1928.

Though the year was a leap year, it did not seem to leap for Elna. Days, and particularly evenings, passed with more quiet than Elna often enjoyed.

In Europe the days of the years 1927 and 1928 were mixed where quiet and excitement were concerned. The big wedding for Dagmar and Lago in early 1928 provided for a good deal of the excitement - mostly in anticipation of the event. Weddings for the other Laumark children, were they to take place, would not take place in Denmark. In addition to Elna and Christine, who sailed for America in 1922, three other Laumark children had left Denmark - all at varying intervals in 1926. Karna had preceded Carl Viggo Laumark and his brother Martin, who traveled together in late October of 1926.

The departure of three family members provided for some tugging at the heart strings and made some days seem longer than they normally would have been. The heart was having a hard time accepting, even if the mind could, that "Laumark" - the family farm - could not support *Bedstemor* and *Bedstefar* and four sons, to say nothing of any family those sons surely would have. If there was excitement, much of that excitement lay in the anticipation of letters from America which

88

would assure the remaining Laumarks in Denmark that each of the children was healthy and was faring well in the new land.

Reports of their newfound work were especially welcomed. Carl and Jensine were pleased to know that all had found work soon after their arrival in the new land. Now and again there were reports of romance for those offspring of Carl and Jensine Laumark who joined Elna and Christine in the new land in the late twenties and that was exciting.

Also important to the Denmark family members were reports on Uncle Rudolf and *Moster* Karen and Uncle Peder and *Tante* Marie. (Karen and Peder were siblings of Jensine.) Both families lived in South River, New Jersey, and had played an important role in settling the young people in the land of opportunity.

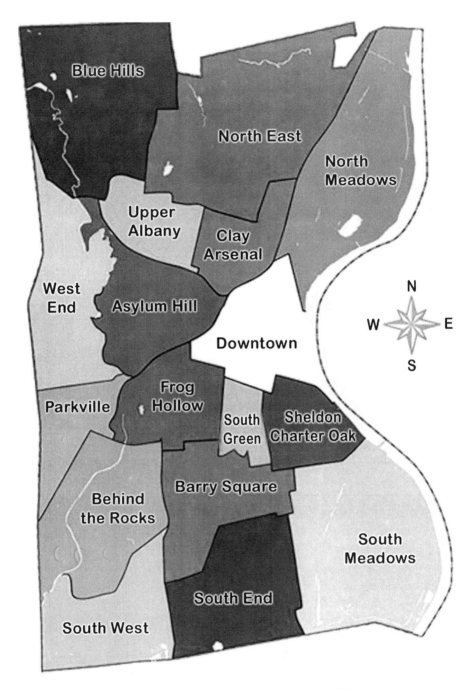

Hartford map showing Frog Hollow

The Years
of Challenge

The Year Was 1929

If the year 1928 seemingly lazed along for Elna, the pace changed dramatically in 1929. A wedding took place in early 1928 - in Denmark, a wedding that did not change much in America for Elna and others of the Laumark family. The year 1929 also started with a wedding, of which there were to be three before the year ended - all of them in America, and that fact served to enliven the year considerably as it moved on.

Carl Viggo (called only "Viggo" - to distinguish him from his father who had the same first name), next in line after Elna, had met a young woman shortly after his arrival in New Jersey in 1926. Marie Trimborn enjoyed life to the fullest. Of German parentage she knew what *gemütlichkeit* meant. It was a joyous celebration of life with lively music, dancing with a hop and a beverage for the "rest" periods between hops at a nearby pub. A man who demonstrated a good sense of humor, Viggo enjoyed all of the moments at that same nearby *Nachtlokale* where good times in Germany were discussed with much laughter especially when the "hardship" times experienced "at home" were recalled - "the good old days" in Germany, they called them.

Viggo was not a stranger to "the good old days" of long days and hard labor. In fact, Viggo's employment in New Jersey was more of the same of what he experienced in Denmark - with a different format, of course. In Denmark he had spent long hours in farming. In America he was a construction worker in the highway development program of the State of New Jersey where he "puddled concrete" from sun-up to sun-down - plus anything else that resembled hard work. "Vik's" reputation was that he was "the hardest working fool" on the whole crew. When he returned home from that kind of a day, he found relief in the nearby establishment where Marie came to help the men laugh at their hardships and to work off the soreness of tired bodies with dances that seemed to take no effort at all.

There was something special about Marie. She was "in step" with the music, but more importantly "in tune" with Viggo's innermost feelings. Those feelings harbored a good deal of pain - pain that was camouflaged by his apparent love of things funny. At the table where the two young people shared in good German fare there was animated exchange between the two of them, but on the dance floor there was intimacy, sharing, and yes, a growing love for one another.

A wedding was held on March 23, 1929 with the nearby Roman Catholic priest presiding. Martin, Viggo's brother, was best man and Elinor Trimborn, Marie's sister-in-law, was matron of honor.

Later in the year on October 26, 1929, the remaining two weddings were held. Karna, who had moved to Connecticut shortly after her arrival in America, became acquainted with a Schlesvig-Holsteiner - Christian Carstensen, a handsome young man with a disarming smile. Chris and Karna courted largely at the Danish Brotherhood Hall in Hartford with much of the same kind of atmosphere that prevailed at the *Nachtlokale* in South River, New Jersey, where Viggo and Marie met. The wedding was held at Our Savior's Danish Lutheran Church in Hartford with Pastor Henning Lund-Sorensen presiding.

The other wedding also held on October 26 was that of Anton Nielsen and Christine Laumark. Anton Nielsen was somewhat older than Christine and had been married previously, but like the younger men, Anton was very enamored with his bride-to-be. Energetic, beautiful and practical she was just what Anton had desired in a wife, homemaker and mother to anticipated children. Anton and Christine were married at the St. Stephens Danish Church in Perth Amboy with New Jersey friends as witnesses. Pastor Peter Goetke presided at the ceremony.

At 144 there was little excitement of the nature just described. To the contrary, time became longer and longer for Elna. The absences on the pretext of "reporting for duty" during the previous year became more frequent and longer as the spring of the year 1929 advanced, and on Monday, June 10, 1929, the absences were given a new explanation. Carl called that evening to announce that he was not returning home. He had found someone else, he said, and advised Elna not to wait for his return. The phone call was short and to the point, with no opportunity for questions to be asked. When the message had been delivered by Carl, there was a click - and SILENCE. It was a silence that was never to be broken. Carl vanished from Elna's life and that of the two children born to the union, vanished on their wedding day.

Elna was numb. If there was any adrenaline, it failed to revive her from her shock. There were many questions, but none of them seemed to register long enough to find an answer. It seemed like she sat in her chair for an eternity, but finally she did go to bed. She did not sleep. She just lay there.

When morning came and her children called for her, Elna hardly had strength to rise to their call. Fortunately, when she did rise, she did not have to answer questions, for Carl had always been gone in the morning before her children awakened. Though the children had never seen her so limp, it did not occur to them that anything "unbelievable" had happened, or that anything had changed. Crawling to their mother for loving support, as they did each morning as they rose to a new day, they served to give more comfort than they received.

Tuesday, June 11, came but created few memories of that day or the day before. Elna did make notes about what needed doing next, but most of the ideas that surfaced were soon scratched out as serving no constructive purpose. The day passed. Evening came and no Carl. By this time there had been many such evenings and the children made no inquiry. They went to bed as they did fairly regularly not seeing their dad. After the children were in bed quiet set in again, but now, a full day later, Elna was able to jot down some things that surely needed doing sometime during the next days.

By the end of the week, Saturday, June 15, Elna embarked on a course with which she had wrestled off and on during the days of that week - still believing that what she had heard in that telephone call was not real. Carl would change his mind and return. But by Saturday the dream seemed to have less and less substance, and she needed to be busy.

Ludins, she remembered, had said to both her and Carl that if they should feel the need for additional income, they could rent out a room. It would be OK. With that thought in her mind, and having run it by her pastor, she knocked on the window of Mr. Ludins' kitchen, hoping to receive his attention. When Jacob Ludins came to the back porch, Elna shared with him what had happened and asked if he would allow the rental of more than one room and if he would be willing to wait for rental money should it turn out that she would not have enough for the July payment of $25.00.

Ludins heard no panic, nor was there any in his own soul. His Jewish religious persuasion had taught him a lot of things about widows and orphans, and the year of residency of the Olsens had taught him some things about the resourcefulness of Elna. He, himself, knew what it was to have a dramatic change in life, first when his daughter was crippled from her fall from the porch and then, again when his wife died after a long illness. With the utmost of calm and with a clear expression of compassion, Ludins assured Elna that he would work with her to overcome this tragedy in her life.

94

The Grief and the Daze of Summer

"Disbelief" was the instant reaction to Carl's phone call. "Surely, he will come home." All of the emotions associated with grief took their turn in Elna's soul. The remaining days of June, (there were twenty of them after Carl called), the hot days of both July and August and well into the month of September were summer days - days which beckoned some outdoor activity (to get out of the house for a change of air and a change of pace). They might well have been labeled "The Daze of Summer." They were filled instead with the full gamut of grief.

Yes, disbelief had been the immediate reaction to Carl's phone call from downtown Hartford, but then came the hurt of rejection. Guilt! What have I done wrong? Bargaining with God. Hope. Surely Carl will return! Anger. Why would he just walk out? He had been gone a lot, but this seemed so final. Despair. What now? All of these feelings and deep, and sometimes hidden, emotions certainly could have earned the term - "the Daze of Summer."

But as Elna grieved, she was not without the knowledge that she had important responsibilities to care for - not least the care of two children, the one age three and the second age one and a half. With her quick wit, she had already decided that renting out more space in her five room flat could bring in revenue which could pay the rent, with perhaps a little left over to provide a few groceries. She had already shared her tragedy with Ludins, the landlord of 142 and 144, who had agreed to work with her.

Elna had had extended experience in caring for children (she had been baby sitter for some of her younger brothers and sisters in Denmark - before she was released for work in a nearby town at age eight.) *Kokkepigens Assistant* was her title, but most things that needed doing were included in the workload and that included the care of children from time to time. Those experiences, together with her hands-on experience with her own children, allowed for a "comfort margin" in her child-caring duties.

Elna's first move, after talking with Ludins, was to arrange a small nine by twelve-foot room with a corner closet which she and Harold and Alice could use as "their" room. The room was adjacent to a room almost twice the size which, as it turned out, served as the kitchen in her flat. While the bedroom was quite crowded, its proximity to the kitchen made it easy for Elna to slip in and out - without bothering the children, if she was very quiet. That left the remaining three rooms as a possibility for rooms to rent.

95

Elna's first contact about filling the available space was her church
- just around the corner. A short chat with Pastor Henning Lund-
Sorensen made it clear that he would help. The two of them had agreed
that there were probably a number of young Danes working in the area
that would like to have a nice, clean place to stay. As he came in contact
with young Danish men, he would make mention of Elna and the
possibility of rental space there, he said. (That thought turned out to be
funny as time passed on). A number of people who needed income and
rented rooms used a different approach from that which Elna
employed. A sign in their windows often said: ROOMS FOR RENT. The
young Danes who passed a number of those signs on their way to Elna's
address could not understand why the rooms in those places would be
declared "TOO CLEAN" - a literal translation from the Danish of "FOR
RENT") From time to time Elna's tragedy was punctuated with
laughter.

Mrs. Hansen, who ran the boarding house in the neighborhood, had
a number of young Danes among her regular customers. That was
Elna's second contact. She had gone there upon Pastor Lund-Sorensen's
suggestion. She had otherwise not known Mrs. Hansen, who never did
have a first name for Elna, even though they lived only five blocks
apart.(Neither of the ladies had time for socializing. They had families
to support). Elna left Mrs. Hansen with the assurance that she would
talk to some of the men who ate at her place.

The Danish Brotherhood was a possible third source, but was
geographically removed from 144 and did not come to play except as
satisfied roomers gave report of "a nice clean place down on Putnam
Street."

A number of would-be renters turned away from 144 after visiting
briefly with Elna. They were looking for a place where they could get
both room and board, they explained, even if that meant staying with an
"American" family - most of whom did not speak English. Like Elna,
most of her neighbors had come from foreign countries and were more
comfortable in their own language - with English as a language of
necessity. Little did those young Danes know that they were going to
get precious little practice in learning the language of their newfound
land in these American homes.

Most of the young Danes who rented anywhere in the
neighborhood, with a variety of arrangements with the providers, had
little intention of continuing in a renting arrangement. They had come
to America for a better life and as opportunities presented themselves,

96

one young Dane after another politely (some not so politely) requested release from his initial longer term commitments. Such had been the experience for Elna, too.

While all of Elna's emotions could have been labeled with that designation, the "Daze of Summer," the "dimensions of grief" were blunted by the demands to get on with life and the care of two children. Running a rooming house served to provide some healing. With men - men from her own culture in the house - there was some protection from the world outside which had different cultural and social expectations which made for a less-than-tranquil feeling in Elna's soul. Occasionally the young Danes could provide the expertise and the brute strength required to fix something or in a desperate moment to run an errand. In a very critical moment they could also look after the children. The fact that their language was one in common with Elna's language, the language of Elna's soul, also served to be a source of comfort for Elna in her difficult time.

Inspite of the demand placed upon her to determine ingenious ways of making a living and the moments of laughter that punctuated her life, there were those moments - not consciously identified as moments of grief - where the pain of separation almost overwhelmed her soul. The dimension of hope returned again and again, following Elna through many years long after the immediate needs of the moment and the lingering pain had become history.

The Immigrant "Boys" from Denmark

"Renting rooms" had not been part of Elna's dream when she had left Denmark in 1922. Her errand had been to chaperon a younger sister on her journey to America to live as "one of theirs" in the home of Peter and Marie Hansen in Sayreville, New Jersey. In fact, living in America for any length of time had not been part of the dream either, but life has a way changing plans - and on a regular basis. And so it did for Elna. In her case the plan to return to Denmark had changed to love and marriage and making a home in America - with Danes, of course, and with one Dane in particular. That change of plans had brought Elna to Hartford, Connecticut, and now to a third address "closer to Carl's work."

"Renting a room" had become part of the plan to move to the third address at 144 Putnam Street, but only for a time long enough to "get us on our feet." The thought would not have been entertained at all, except for the fact that the second floor at 144 had more space than the family would need. "A room" is what Elna had bargained for when she and Carl talked to Jacob Ludins about rental provisions. But now it was "rooms" - two in the beginning and "at most" two. The two rooms in Elna's thinking included the room that she and Carl shared and a sitting room at the front of the house that could be made into a bedroom - with "a curtain to begin with" and later with a "plywood partition with a door built in" for passage to the room. (Another door to the front hallway was available , but it would have meant exiting the apartment to re-enter it to go to the bathroom and that did not seem right.)

It was a very still day near the end of June, when there came a knock at the front door. The knock sounded like a bomb going off. On the other side was a stranger. "I'll look through the keyhole," she said to herself, and she did, but all she could see was the hulk of a man who had backed off slightly after he knocked, but she did not see enough of him to get any idea of who the man might be. "It would have to be a Dane!" "Maybe not!" A significant number of strangers climbed the stairs and walked the hallways where the man stood. Some knocked in the hope of getting a drink or a handout of some sort. Though times were good, a significant number of people in that neighborhood were out of work for one reason or another - most often because of an alcohol problem or some other socially unacceptable behavior.

Elna braced herself. She had, after all, asked her pastor, friends and other Danes to direct renters to her door. Carefully she opened the door and there! There stood Henry Madsen. She did not know him, but he spoke Danish! He was all dressed up and was otherwise extremely well-groomed. (His mother in Denmark had told him that he needed to dress up to be accepted in the new land.) He explained to her that he was from Kolding and that he had come to America to escape the depression in Europe and to gain employment here. He also explained that he had "landed a job" with the Lincoln Dairy over on Ward Place. He had been looking for something closer to his work, but when he heard that there was a place in a Danish home, he thought he would prefer that.

The room rent would be $2.50 a week - in advance, but at that price she would need two people in a room. And - there would be no meals. If that was acceptable, did he know of anyone with whom he could share the room? Elna made it clear that the other person would have to be male and, of course, acceptable to Henry. She would prefer someone Danish, but if he could get along with the person, some other nationality would be O.K. (Elna felt she had already pressed her wishes as far as she could, by asking Henry to find another person to share the room.)

Henry said that he thought he could work out an arrangement with a fellow employee. Would she hold the room (the front room) for him until he had opportunity to inquire of his co-worker? "Yes, of course," was her reply. While the answer spelled out self-assurance, Elna harbored some anxiety about Henry's return. But return, Henry did. In tow, Henry had a man of much smaller stature with kinky blonde hair whose name was Oscar Andersen. Like Henry, Oscar had a route for the delivery of "pasteurized" milk to people who lived in the three and six tenement houses that filled most neighborhoods that were close to the factories in which many of the neighborhood people worked.

Henry had not said anything about the meals which Elna had declared would not be available, but as it turned out both Henry and Oscar had to be at the dairy by 4:00 a.m. to wrestle the milk cases onto their horse-drawn wagons, hitch up the team or a single horse as each wagon would demand and be on the route by 5:00 a.m. for quick delivery to people who needed the milk before they sent family members off to work. The route usually called for a double run - one for those who had to be in the factories at 7:00 a.m. and one for those whose work called for a later hour of arrival - insurance workers and downtown employees who drew their wages from the stores on Main Street or its adjacent streets and avenues. Henry and Oscar had both learned who the people were that fit both categories and were good workers.

But at 3:30 a.m.? (The two men could make it to work on foot if they left at that hour.) Where would they find breakfast? Would it be all right, if they could help themselves with a little breakfast before they left for work? They would pay a little "extra" for that privilege, and Elna would not have to get up to fix anything, they insisted. "Of course," was Elna's reply.

She, now, had two renters. It would not quite take care of Elna's full rent, but with the little "extra" she might be able not only to have food on hand for the "boys," but there might be a little left for her and her children. It helped that the "boys" were given an extra quart of milk for their own use that they brought home and from which Elna could also benefit.

July 1 was imminently upon Elna and she could have paid the rent in full, but there was no assurance that she had solved her problem or that it would be solved by that "rent due" date. A day or two in advance of the "rent due" date, Elna knocked gently on the kitchen window of the Ludins' quarters. She wanted to summon him to share with him the progress that she had made. She also explained that she could pay the rent in full, but that she would be "up against it" where feeding her children was concerned and could he wait a day or two so that she could continue with her rental venture.

Jacob Ludins cared about the welfare of Elna Olsen and her children, and he had already observed that her first renters were gentlemen who gave special attention not to disturb the neighbors in their effort to get to work on time and that they were otherwise gentlemen about everything they did. "Henry has a certain dignity about him," Ludins noted in the exchange that took place across the railings of adjacent back porches. Elna agreed. Henry's Danish mother had prepared him well for life and yes, for success in the new land called "America."

100

Rooms for Rent with Strength from God

Henry Madsen and Oscar Andersen had hardly settled in at 144 when Karna, Elna's sister, came to ask if she could stay in the other bedroom. She had landed a job at Merrow Machine Company, on the banks of the Park "Hog" River where Underwood Typewriter Company and several other manufacturing firms were located. Merrow Machine was within very easy walking distance from 144. Karna had been living with a couple of single women with whom she had made acquaintance at the Danish Brotherhood Hall on White Street. Though a bus made its way to the inner city from the White Street Hall, passing within walking distance to the Merrow Machine Company, there had been no pay at the point at which Karna came to Elna for permission to stay. Bus fare was out of the question. While rental "without payment in advance" violated Elna's rules, she was sure that she would be paid (the only terms which could be acceptable under the circumstances). With three beds filled, Elna could "make it" if she was very careful. From Karna she also received a little pay for meals, so that Karna did not have to buy expensive meals in the eating establishments nearby - another variation from the established rules which included "no meals."

Seven dollars and fifty cents each week would pay the rent each month with five dollars to spare for the other necessities of raising a family at 144. The remaining amount was not enough, but there were other things that Elna could do, and did - hospice sitting, for instance. On Putnam Heights Street on the second floor of number fifteen was a family that had been looking for someone to sit with Mrs. Chretien, who was terminally ill with cancer. Elna felt fortunate to be able to get something that close. And Mr. Chretien, who worked from 7:00 a.m. to 4:30 p.m. each day at the Underwood Typewriter Company, was much relieved to have someone there to minister to his wife's needs. The work was not ideal for a woman with two children who had to be part of the arrangement, but it worked because Elna's children somehow knew that they needed to help for those several hours each day. Having already earned a reputation as a seamstress in the neighborhood, Elna usually had tailoring that she could do while she was at the Chretien home, and there was time between 4:45 p.m. each day and *aftensmad* to do a little shopping over on Park Street before going home.

Saturdays were busy days. Bed sheets from three rental beds plus those which Elna and her children used needed to be laundered - in the wash tubs, already in place in the kitchen of her flat, in the early stages. Later these were replaced by a used Maytag with an electric motor and a manually operated wringer. The clothesline which spanned the backyard from Elna's backporch to a pole at the end of the backyard sagged under the load each week. In the winter the sheets became frozen stiff and had to be ironed dry before being placed on the beds.

Sundays were given to a short walk to Our Savior's Danish Lutheran Church. From the worship services there, Elna received her strength for the following week and sometimes an agreement with one of her fellow Danes "to make something that we can send to Denmark to our family there." At Our Savior's she also learned that there were Danes there who were casting off clothing which marked the Danes as "immigrants." She could make something for her children to wear, and she could sometimes sell something to a neighbor who would benefit from custom fitting. Her fellow worshippers were glad to share their castoffs with Elna. "Maybe it could help a little," they would say. And, of course, there was Pastor Henning Lund-Sorensen who had counseled her through some very difficult days following the departure of Carl in mid-June of 1929.

Filled with determination and with *godt helbred* (good health) going for her, Elna did what needed doing to care for herself and her two children.

But all did not always go well for her. A crowning blow came in early 1930 when Pastor Henning Lund-Sorensen announced to the congregation that he was resigning and returning to Denmark where he felt more at home in his call to be a pastor. Headquarters for "the church in America" was in Des Moines, and the church was still struggling for the kind of identity it would have in America. The Benton Street Church (*Den Forenede Kirke i USA*) was loathed to join the Grundtvigians in Our Savior's Church. Had they been able to join Our Savior's, the congregation on Russ and Babcock Streets could have been a more viable church, and there might have been a good reason to stay in America longer, but under the circumstances, being a pastor in Denmark was more secure and language which had been something of a barrier would not be the barrier that it was for him in the U.S.A. For Elna, there was a feeling of abandonment - a second such experience in less than a year.

Fortunately for Elna, she was busy enough so that there was little time to dwell on disappointments (or even abandonments). Caring for herself and her two children used up all of the energy that she had. Wet

102

handkerchiefs, if there had been time to make them wet, found no place with bedsheets and other laundry that was ever a part of her days and nights at the turn of the decade from 1929 to 1930.

Pastors from other parts of District I of the Danish Evangelical Lutheran Church in America came from time to time to help the congregation with its needs - needs that were covered by a number of lay people with strong faith commitments and who were dedicated not to let this little Danish island of faith succumb to the hard times that had a way of appearing every now and then, both for the congregation and for various individuals in it.

The vacancy at Our Savior's was fairly short. By the fall of 1930 there was to be a new pastor - a "farmer" many of the members said (not a compliment - quite the contrary). He was from someplace out west - "Iowa, I tink," said one. "Yah!" said another, "Out der vaer the Daniss College iss. He's probably goin' to be awl right!" The man of whom they spoke with critical curiosity was Valdemar S. Jensen - a giant of a man and a giant of the faith, "filled with both physical and spiritual strength." "A man for deez times," said those who were party to getting him to Hartford, Connecticut. "He speeks boadt Daniss and Engliss. Dat shouldt be gudt for oss," said a member who denied on a regular basis that he was from Denmark or any other part of Europe for that matter.

The 1930s were to be difficult years, but rarely with any despair. Each day was a new day with challenges and opportunities. Each day was to be a day with the world and with God.

The Great Depression Years at 144

Karna's stay with Elna was short-lived. Arriving as she did in mid July of 1929, Karna closed her stay at 144 with her marriage in late October of the same year at Our Savior's Lutheran Church to Chris Carstensen from Schlesvig Holstein. There had been some thought that the newlyweds would stay at 144, but with rent increasing from Karna's $2.50 to $5.00 by virtue of her marriage to Chris, it was decided that the newly married couple should have an apartment of their own. They found a place on the third floor on Zion Street at Ward Place.

From that location Karna could still walk to work at Merrow Machine, though the distance was more than doubled that from 144 to Merrow Machine. Chris, in any case, would have to take the bus to the center of Hartford, where he would transfer to a bus that would take him to the Hartford Electric Light Co. where he had found employment as an apprentice electrician.

Taking Karna's place at Elna's was a younger brother of the two sisters. Peter had come to the United States shortly before Christmas in 1929, but had gone to South River, New Jersey, to be with his eldest brother, Viggo, until he could find work. A gentle man, Peter was not given to joining his elder brother in construction work, and little else seemed to present itself to him. Like the two sisters before him who had lived in New Jersey, he moved to Hartford, where with the help of his sister, Karna, he also found employment at the Merrow Machine Company - sweeping floors at first and on to jobs throughout the factory that required more brain power.

To help him with the latter work, Peter enrolled in English classes in special education programs developed by the city of Hartford and its industries to assist newcomers in the language of their newfound country and to assist them in other areas which would be helpful in making adjustments. With his keen mind and quick wit, Peter learned the English language. Of the seven Laumarks who came to the United States, he was the only one who learned to speak English with little evidence of having come from Europe.

Almost simultaneously with Karna's departure as a renter in Elna's plan, Henry Madsen declared in mid-September that he would be moving by the end of the month. New employment for him made living at 144 less than convenient. He was giving notice, so that she could look around a bit for someone who could share the room that he had shared with Oscar Andersen. Waiting in the wings for the opportunity was an elder brother of Oscar's - Gustav, who was a house painter. The two brothers would be compatible, said Oscar, and so they were, solving Elna's problems for the moment.

With fall approaching, a new problem in renting presented itself. The front room, now occupied by the Andersen brothers, had no heat. Central heat and central air was an unheard of idea when 142 and 144 were built. Provision had been made, however, for venting a space heating stove. The Andersens were welcome to stay, Elna said, but she would need an increase in rent to $3.00 to provide for heating the room. The choice was theirs, of course, but there was little hesitation on the part of either brother. Living on Putnam Street and living with Elna with her efficient and pleasant manner was "woert evri pennie!" they said.

The Andersens could have a say in what kind of stove would be the best and with one accord, Elna and the two young brothers decided on an oil stove - no ashes to carry out, they were quick to add. With a second floor flat and winter sure to come, the boys wanted no part of carrying ashes to the "ash shed" which was at the back of the lot, behind the house. Oil (kerosene) it was.

Sharing the room with Peter from time to time were his brothers, Martin and Ejner Christian, recent immigrants like all the others of the Laumark family (seven in all). Martin, also a gentle soul, could not find acceptable work because of some early problems in learning the language, and he returned quickly to New Jersey to join his brother Viggo in construction. Ejner Christian (affectionately called "Kisse" by his mother in Denmark) was brilliant but of a fickle temperament. No job suited him. He came and went until it was clear that he could make it in the painting business in New Jersey.

Family members were asked to be responsible for their time with Elna and were fairly regular when employment was available to them. From time to time there were some IOUs, but for the most part payment was made in a timely fashion.

With young Danes occupying 144 - on the second floor - as they did, many young Danish men came from time to time, not to rent rooms, but to find warmth and coziness, and to play cards or checkers (the least expensive entertainment that they could think of). Most of the time, the young men were very gentlemanly, but on occasion strong opinions prevailed and there was need to remind them that in the building where they were gathered were twenty-six other individuals who occupied the other five units of the building. A little reminder settled the young men into the quiet mode which they had promised to keep.

105

Conversation, as these young Danes talked with each other, was often hilarious! In Denmark there had been few cars in their experience, but now in the United States there were not only cars, but there was a variety of makes - many of which were invented and/or developed in Connecticut. Now and again, there would be mention of the Stanley Steamer (pre-internal combustion days). Autos propelled by battery powered engines made an appearance on occasion. Their dream always was that one day they would own an automobile.

"But dey er expensive!" one would proclaim. "You gotta keep dem op!" another would chime. "Ja!" said still another, "You gotta buy new 'rubbers' for them once in a while and dat costs money!" Automobile tires were made of rubber, and the men understood that. On occasion the English word for "tire" did not come quickly to mind, so the word "rubber" had to do. "Ja! Dis is a crazie language!" they would exclaim. "Jeg har en 'kloer' knecht! Og saa er den min!" The card game would be over, and with the same determination that dominated their card game, they quietly departed 144 with a Danish song in their hearts.

"It's Me! Elna"

It was 9:40 p.m. on a Friday in the late fall of 1929 when there was a knock on the main door to Elna's flat at 144. In intervals of a few seconds the knock got louder until it was that Elna, ironing sheets in the kitchen, heard it. "Who in all of the world would knock this late at night?" she thought.

Disturbing the men who regarded their rooms as their private quarters and who slept soundly after early morning hours and long days of work did not seem just right for Elna. Having also heard, besides the knock, that Harold had not fully succumbed to sleep, Elna decided to enlist Harold's help (He was almost four years old). He could cry out for help, if the would be intruder did not turn out to be a friend. Carefully Harold followed his mother to the front end of her rented space where the main door was located, passing through a corridor which linked the two ends of the flat to each other.

Quietly they stood inside the main door waiting for the next knock which they were sure would shortly come. "Who is it?" said Elna. "It's me, Elna," said the voice on the other side of the door. "It's me. *Lille* Pete!" he said with muted pride. "I'll step back from the door, so that you can see me through the keyhole, if you wish," he continued. "But you will hardly know me! I haven't shaved for two weeks. My clothes are dirty and filled with lice. I have walked from California - there is no work there either," he said.

Already the effect of the market collapse of late 1929 had made its mark across the land "where the streets are paved in gold." Local folks, mostly, could find something to do, but transients?" No, there is no work here," signs would say at every farm road and at every city limit. The desert was devoid of population and industry, and California was filled with people who were sure that in that land of gold there would be something.

Lille Pete could document the entire journey, if not on paper, then in his memory and now he stood at Elna's door - a place where he had stood before when he came to visit with the men who roomed at 144 and where they played cards and talked of their fantasies about a "new life" in a "new land."

"Do you have anything to eat? I am hungry," he said with some evidence of pain. " But, before I come in I am going down to the police station to shave and to shower. Maybe I can find some different clothing there too. I will be back in about 40 minutes or so!"

Elna was stunned, not only by what she heard and saw, but by her own awareness of a pantry that was sparsely supplied. Her numbness was short lived as she thought of a possible place where *Lille* Pete might lie down for the night. "Of course," she said, " I will help you." Then Elna continued, "And you, Harold! You have been a good boy. You can go to bed again now."

Lille Pete performed as he had promised. When he returned, he looked better, he smelled better, and his very good sense of humor had returned. The thought of sleeping indoors appealed to him as did the thought that he might get some "real" food.

Elna, on the otherhand, also performed as promised. "You can sleep here in the living room on the couch," she said. "I do not have much food - only a little bite for Henry and Oscar before they go off to work at 3:30 tomorrow morning. They are milkmen, and they leave early to harness the horses and to load their wagons for their morning deliveries. If you promise not to eat it all, you can have a little of what they usually get until they can eat a real breakfast later," Elna continued.

"Oh, I am so grateful," *Lille* Pete said. "And I promise! You just go off to bed with your children. Thanks. Many thousand thanks. You are a wonderful woman!"

Sleep, Elna did - however short the night - arising at 3:00 a.m. to get food out for Henry and Oscar before their departure for work. There was evidence that *Lille* Pete had eaten, and a look into the pantry made it clear that he had not kept his promise. The breakfast food was gone. All of it! Even that which she had planned for her children, Harold and Alice.

Elna's greatest fear was that the two men at the front of the house would awaken and that there would be some loud fussing because there was no food to start them out on their commitment for the day. Her fear was unnecessary. The men slept soundly past the hour they were to arise. And, quickly, Elna decided that she would let them sleep - declaring in the last moment that they had overslept and that, if they hurried, they could still make it to work on time.

There was little thought on the part of Henry and Oscar of eating any breakfast under the circumstances, and without ever noticing *Lille* Pete who they passed on the way to the bathroom they dashed out of the tenement building and on to Ward Place. A bottle of whole milk later had to hold them until their usual breakfast time.

What Elna knew, in addition to the fact that she had cleverly handled her difficult moment, was that her brother Peter would be returning from his work at 8:30 a.m. with a pay envelope in hand - ready to pay his rent (which he did in weekly installments), and with his money she could make it to Park Street in time to purchase something for the children for their breakfast.

At 6:00 a.m. *Lille* Pete awakened. He knew he had pressed his luck the night before. Quickly he cleaned up and left 144 in search of his next day's meal and nighttime shelter. Before leaving, he ventured out briefly to the kitchen to say: *"Tak! Uendlig tak for alt!"* (Thanks! Yes, thanks for everything.)

One more chapter had passed for Elna in a difficult life in America - a life that was to have many chapters in the days and years that lay ahead for her at 144 - and more.

A Man of Power and Might

The Great Depression was well under way in 1930, and Hartford, Connecticut, was not to be spared. More and more young Danes who had come to Hartford appeared at the "nice clean place down on Putnam Street" with a request for a night or two of lodging "until they could find something." One by one they came. Andersen, Bendiksen, Lynne, Begtrup, Kirkegaard, Rasmussen, Plough, Tilstrup, Moeller, Jensen and Petersen. One after another, Danish men came, often appealing to their place of origin in Denmark, hoping to find a tender spot in the heart of Elna and a bed "for only one night" at the "nice clean place."

Occasionally there would be a Rasmussen or a Hansen who would return to report that not only had he found a place to stay, but that he had found some kind of work to generate the money he needed to pay for his keep. Every now and then, a new man would find his way in to play cards and/or chess and by virtue of a generous heart of one already housed at 144, a place to lay down "for only a few minutes, Elna!"

"He didn't stay long," would be the statement when Elna inquired about the longer than usual visit. "You won't have to wash the sheets, Elna," one would say, and "I wasn't using the bed just then anyhow," followed the announcement about sheets.

Mr. Ludins, the landlord, winked at the traffic! He was very much aware of the need to give compassion to those in need. Every now and then he commented to Elna about what a wonderful lady she was and how understanding she seemed to be about the needs of people - especially those who had severed their roots from families in distant European and Mediterranean lands. Danes, it seemed, were less rowdy than some of those from other heritages - at least, he thought so, as he spoke.

But not all who came to visit Elna were there to extract a favor. In a few instances those who came were there to bestow a favor or to issue some other kindness.

Among those men was a "giant" of a man. Tall. Elegant in stature. Pleasant. A man with dignity and authority. That man was Pastor Valdemar S. Jensen - the newly called pastor of Our Savior's Danish Lutheran Church about whom the members of the congregation had talked earlier when he was called to serve in Hartford. As it turned out, Pastor Jensen was the man for the hour, though not all enjoyed him. His strong faith was especially evident when he rose in his pastoral robe at the worship hour to ask those who came to the church service to rise and confess with him their faith in the Triune God (The Apostles Creed - *Trosbekendelsen*)

Beginning always with the renunciation of the Devil and all his works and all his ways, he began:

Vi forsager Djævelen og alle hans gerninger og alle hans væsen!
Vi tror paa Gud Fader, Himlens og Jordens Skaber.

With his very strong voice he stomped out sin and the Devil, and declared his faith in a God for all ages and for all circumstances.

As he stood tall in the pulpit at Russ and Babcock Streets in a church that revealed the reverence of faithful Danes in its architecture and the beauty of its stained glass windows, it was as if God Himself had come to share - not condemnation, but hope, power, and new life for those who had come to *Amerika* for a new beginning.

The pulpit from which Valdemar Sejr Jensen preached the gospel was decorated with a golden fringe around the top, and as he preached Pastor Jensen's fingers played with that fringe as if to give musical emphasis to what was being said. And only Jensen could raise his head to the heavens and give the powerful impression that he was in direct communication with God - the God who had important words for His people - about being God's creatures, about being Danish, about being talented, about being productive and generous, about hope in a dark hour for every workingman and for a nation seeking to build its full identity as a leader among nations and among men. Each time Pastor Jensen raised his hand from the pulpit keyboard which he played, a blessing fell upon the humble worshippers who sat below in the pew.

In Sunday School as he told the Bible stories, they came alive for *kidzener* - and if Goliath thought he had a combatant in David, he would have abdicated under this giant of a man who delivered righteousness with power and might.

All of the above applied to the new pastor called to lead the sheep at *"Vor Frelsers Dansk Evangeliske Kirke i Hartford, Connecticut."* So also did his kindness to his people. He had just come from a period in his life when he himself had worked hard for a living - working as he did for his brother Thorvald C. Jensen, contractor, puddling concrete and building bridges in the sweltering and freezing temperatures of Iowa, learning from his fellow workers what hard living was all about. A man of great learning he joined many who did not have that privilege, and he seized on the opportunity of learning from them about the "hard work" of making a living.

Together with his working partner, his wife Lene, he listened to the life stories of hundreds of Danes who had left their families and who had no place to go to share their grief and their sorrow. Young people, the age of his own sons of whom there were four, unwittingly unloaded their pain and wittingly shared their joy in the parsonage which stood next to the church.

As a symbol of God in the midst of a people on a journey of life, he was called upon to represent the saving God in a tremendous variety of life situations and styles.

"O, du skal ha' tak Gud fordi du kom," (Oh God, you deserve thanks because you have come) was a thought entertained in the hearts of many Hartford Danes - perhaps especially those who came from the peasant families and townships of Jylland, because Pastor Valdemar Jensen represented God in their lives.

"I am going down to see the pastor," Elna often declared. Sometimes the visit was motivated by the need for counsel. At other times the visit was motivated by a great joy that quite often comes to the people who await God's presence in their lives.

Sunday and Other Visitors

Pastor Valdemar S. Jensen was not the only one who came from Our Savior's Danish Lutheran Church to visit Elna at 144. Though his study was not far from 144, his visits did not occur often. Other pastoral duties kept him busy. There were others. Many of those others were those who lived long distances from the church and who seldom had an opportunity to visit with people who shared their values and their faith. Sunday afternoon seemed to provide such an opportunity.

Members of Our Savior's Danish Lutheran Church (and that included all Danes who were baptized in the Church of Denmark, whether on the *medlemmers* list or not), were scattered throughout central Connecticut and a round trip to church was at least a half day's journey. By taking advantage of an afternoon with immigrant friends, who like themselves, hungered to share their experiences of being in a new land, they found a meaningful way to spend the rest of the day.

Elna's flat was just around the corner from Our Savior's and became one of the places where people could find comfort and the freedom to exchange their experiences of the past and their hopes about the future. Elna's flat was also on the bus line, from which bus line visitors to 144 could transfer to other buses or trolleys to their home destinations. That was also a very much welcomed convenience.

Among those who stopped often were Victor and Jenny Holt, a very proper couple who did not have the good fortune of having children who needed their attention. They enjoyed visiting with Elna and, as importantly, Elna's children. The couple was doing better than average where employment was concerned. Both of them worked. Victor had secured a position as the driver of a hearse for a funeral home in the city, whose services were always needed - even in hard times. Jenny was a hairdresser in one of the beauty shops in central Hartford. Vic hardly had to explain his work. His uniform for his position (a black suit and tie with a stiffly starched white shirt) suggested the nature of his work. His chauffeur's cap, in contrast to the cab drivers of the city, was hexagonal in shape and suggested high station among those who drove for others - living or dead. Jenny's preoccupation with beauty and beautifying others was made clear by her own dress, none of which suggested poverty. "Efter all," the more vocal Danes would note, "They have two jobs!" At Elna's they could take off their cap and let down their hair.

Jakob and Bertine Norregaard were among the frequent visitors. Unionville was their home community - about eight miles west of

Hartford, beyond the Avon Mountains. A street car ran every hour on the hour during the workweek for people who worked in the factories and other enterprises in Hartford, East Hartford and West Hartford. On Sundays the streetcar also ran on the hour, but only until 2:00 p.m. for the outbound run. Service picked up again at 6:00 p.m. allowing the bus drivers and the trolley operators time to visit with their own families on that day before delivering those who had ridden with them to the city.

Jakob was retired from the Minneapolis Park Department and had settled in Unionville on a few acres which were purchased by the Danish Young People of central Connecticut and on which they established a retreat center for all of the young Danes in central Connecticut. Lectures in Danish, folk dancing, gymnastics and hiking were all part of the fare at "*Vennelejr*," as their place was called. It was a "dusting for their souls," but no place for sofa lovers except for the occasional lectures which were offered, sometimes long enough to require seating.

Bertine and Elna chatted with great animation about folk dancing and the physical feats related to gymnastics, while Jakob seized on an opportunity to close his eyes for a little nap.

Marie Back often stopped by even though to return home from church by way of Putnam Street lengthened her trip. With a good sense of humor, she enjoyed Elna and especially Elna's children. A recognized nurse in Denmark, Marie grew up in an orphanage (*børnehjem*) and emigrated to America in the late teens of the twentieth century. Shortly thereafter she took up with John Back, a *Thyboer*, and established with him a dairy behind their two-story home where they pasteurized milk brought to them by nearby dairy farmers and from where the milk was delivered to the various neighborhoods of the city of Hartford. A bachelor brother, Fred, lived with them and worked in the business. There were no children in the Back home. Harold and Alice, Elna's two, became special to this lady, whose laughter of joy rang for blocks around.

There was a steady stream of visitors on Sunday of those who came to see and to share with Elna. It was a different group from the stream of visitors that came to visit "the boys" who rented sleeping space from Elna. Those who came on Sunday were more taken up with matters of faith and culture than were the other visitors who were more preoccupied with their various occupations and games. Elna thoroughly enjoyed the Sunday visitors.

In addition to the occasional visits from the pastor and the regular visits of the Sunday worshippers and the lonesome boys from Denmark

114

who came during the week, there was a surprise visitor one afternoon - "with an errand." This visitor was Chris Jensen.

Chris Jensen was a little man, but he was not short on genius. His visit was not a social one. It was a business call. After a very modest meal at Mrs. Hansen's boarding house he walked to 144 and with determination knocked vigorously on Elna's door. Upon gaining admission to Elna's flat, Chris stated his case succinctly. He needed to borrow a shirt, he said - a white shirt - and he had learned at Mrs. Hansen's that several men roomed at Elna's and that surely one of them would have a white shirt he could borrow and one that would fit him. Chris was in pursuit of a job - in sales - and he needed a white shirt to get the job, he said. Could he borrow a shirt for his interview, he asked. "I will have it washed and ironed and returned to you in just two hours," he said. "Your tenant does not even need to know that the shirt was gone," he explained.

Elna was reluctant. Only one man had a white shirt that would fit Chris for his purposes. That shirt belonged to Oscar Andersen. With his persuasive charm, Chris convinced Elna that what he and she would be up to would essentially go unnoticed. Won over by his charm, Elna joined him in his job hunting conspiracy. Chris got the shirt, and it was returned promptly as he had promised.

Had he gotten the job, Elna asked. "Yes," said Chris with a smile. He was to be an auto salesman. Chrysler would be his product.

Of Sunday visitors there were many. Of weekday visitors there were regulars. Of surprise visits there were few. But all of the visits to 144 left little, or no, opportunity for boredom or time to dwell on any misfortunes which may have come into her life. If, and when, the moments of pain made their way through Elna's busy life, it was a short walk down to visit with Pastor Jensen and his wife, Lene.

Room Rental and Avon Products

Renting sleeping space - "bed and bath" - provided some rather irregular income for Elna. Though her rooms and beds usually had takers, many of the renters came and went as circumstances dictated. Sometimes it was a job that did not survive the deep depression of the 1930s. Sometimes it was love and marriage. Sometimes it was failure to budget properly. Though not frequent, IOUs took the place of cash - some lasting only a few day; others weeks. The parade of renters was regular - with some staying a relatively long time and others staying for a week or ten days.

Among those who rented, the Andersen brothers, Gustav and Oscar, stayed the longest. For several years they shared the front room of the flat. Oscar had steady employment with the Lincoln Dairy, but Gustav was a house painter and people put off their paint jobs as long as they could - often leaving Gus sitting at home, experimenting with his abilities to be a fine artist.

Others, like Gus, also found their employment somewhat unreliable. They joined Gus in his idle time, playing checkers and a variety of card games. They mused a great deal about their station in America, knowing full well that there had been good cause to leave Denmark when they did. While they passed time, they often discussed the ethics of being semi-employed foreigners and how some of their acquaintances cut corners to make it in the new land. From time to time there was a pontifical statement about that behavior, "Why, dey couldt get deported for dat!"

Their idle hours also served as learning hours for Elna's children, who were quite welcome to listen in and watch the proceedings. The children learned the language and the proceedings well - so well that Elna needed to give lessons in behavior to grown men who had become role models for the children who were welcome in their midst.

On several occasions Elna heard her children from another room as they played cards and checkers. In either instance they had learned that some plays required exclamation, filled with the emotions of having played or moved in error. When she went to find out what the children were doing, she learned that, like the men, they moved the checkers each time carefully applying a word of profanity with the move." How to change that course?" she mused. In thinking about it she decided to invite the boys in to watch her children play their games. It took only a few words of profanity to teach the boys that they needed to play their games with a bit more restraint.

116

Elna often noted that their play improved with the curbing of their language. She was pleased at the lessons learned by all concerned.

With income being as erratic as it was for the boys, Elna shared in the same difficulty of making ends meet. Rent was as regular as the calendar. Groceries for her and her children were a daily need. Shoes seemed to wear out with regularity. As Elna reflected on her circumstances, she concluded that there was time that could be translated into income or making what income she had, last longer.

She had learned from some of her neighbor ladies that "you can make good money selling Avon products." Earlier she could not consider that kind of work for several reasons. She could not afford the inventory. Her children could not walk the sometimes long distances for the deliveries which were required. Taking the bus or streetcar to make deliveries soon turned a job in which "you can make good money" into one that made little money. But now her children were old enough to be part of the shorter distances for delivery.

It was only about three-quarters of a mile on Park Street to service some of those who bought her products, and the children liked to go on that journey. A.C. Petersen's Dairy Ice Cream Store was on the way, and sometimes when the sales were big enough, there would be ice cream. Riding on the bus or the street car also provided some fascination when it was calculated that such a trip could produce a profit.

The experiment did not last long. Keeping track of orders and maintaining books often came late at night and exhaustion threatened accuracy in both departments. As it turned out it did not provide adequate profit or enjoyment for the energy expended.

"Do it yourself" projects, while they did not make any money, often saved money and with careful planning Elna put enough money away to buy a used White Sewing Machine. Her fellow worshippers at the church were considerate and made available to her castoff garments which could be converted to clothing for her children. Warm woolen coats and other garments came off the old White Machine filling needs for attire that arose from time to time.

Word of mouth recommendations informed a number of people that Elna was handy with a sewing machine. Making alterations and new garments became part of Elna's routine to care for herself and her children. People came and went as Elna had time, bringing not only the cloth which she should sew but also news of the outside world to a lady who was fairly well confined to her home and her workplace.

Much of Elna's concern for making a living diminished with the passing of the most difficult of the depression years. A non-Dane

117

lightened her burden when upon application for sleeping space at 144 declared that he would like to rent the "front" room - the room vacated by the Andersen brothers. He would pay double rent and would buy the fuel for winter occupancy. He was seeking privacy and comfort, he said, and with his offer he felt that he would be able to have both.

George's offer, while generous, was in his own interest as well. It was only two blocks to his work at the Hartford Machine Screw Company where he was a toolmaker. He was only blocks from eating establishments for all of his meals. His social life, which was centered mostly in those establishments could be continued and amplified over what it had been when he lived at a residence that required public transportation.

Washing sheets and towels for one person - a person who was always neat and clean - lightened the load at 144. George's amiable personality - almost charismatic - superceded that of some of those who had paid the rent in the earlier years of Elna's endeavors to survive in a difficult time in her life.

The World Outside Elna's Place

Much of Elna's life in the late 20s and the early 30s centered in her home and in her church. Both were essentially Danish, a fact that brought a great sense of security to a young mother trying to develop support for herself and for her two children, but outside of those two communities there was a whole other world.

In the tenement building itself, designated as 142 and 144 Putnam Street, there were six families representing the Catholic, Jewish and Protestant religious groups. In addition to the residents of the building, there were the people who came with regularity to the neighborhood store which occupied the first floor at 142.

Owners and residents of the unit which housed the neighborhood store were Mr. and Mrs. Solo, Russian Orthodox Jews. Hard working people and religiously devout, they spoke only enough English to deal with the people who traded with them, who, in turn, spoke only enough English to buy the basic necessities for homemaking in the neighborhood. What these people believed, which was a mystery to most of the people of the neighborhood, became recognized by all as the great significance of the Sabbath. This was especially true among the children who were regularly enlisted to light the candles on the menorah shortly after 6:00 p.m. on Friday - the beginning of the Sabbath when no work was to be done including whatever work was involved in lighting candles. Young people who entered the Solo living quarters were intrigued by the strange goings-on in that place. A gentile was employed to cover the business activity of Saturday for all the other gentiles who all knew that the Sabbath was Sunday.

Above the store lived Mr. Ludins with his crippled daughter. They were also Jews but not of the orthodox variety. They honored the Sabbath and all of the other Jewish holy days, but in a more relaxed manner. No religious prohibitions were violated and their life-style was not religiously severe in the eyes of on-lookers. Honesty and integrity and compassion were among their chief virtues.

On the third floor over the store was the Patrick Hagen family - Irish Catholics. Big brother Ed was entering his teens, presenting the family with some difficulty. Pat, Jr. was about the same age as Harold and tagged along regularly with his tricycle to shopping on Park Street - only two blocks away. The tricycle was a peace offering to all of the members of the family who suffered from inadequate support attributable to a drinking problem on the part of Pat, Senior.

Below Elna's quarters were the Murphys - thirteen of them. They scrambled to make enough money "to buy shoes and put food on the table." Mary, the eldest of the eleven offspring, had a good education (a high school diploma) and a job at the bank as a teller. Margaret, still had a year in school, but she helped with part time waitress jobs at the local pubs - eating establishments featuring every kind of fare cooked in peasant homes of the Europe from whence their owners had come. Bill was also the same age as Harold, and Irene, the youngest, was still in diapers, or dragging one, on the well-worn floor of that flat.

Upstairs from Elna was Mary O'Malley, a twice married Irish Catholic, with four sons - Maury, John, and Ted, all Flannigans by a father who died while the boys were growing up, and Edward O'Malley, a son by her second husband. Maury, the eldest, and Eddie, the youngest, provided what little support that Mary had for her rocking chair existence. A little stimulant from a corked bottle beside her, kept a smile on her face in her great stress of surviving with her four sons. "Oh, Me hips!" she would exclaim on occasion - mostly when the barometer changed and the "medicinal" drink beside her was nearly gone. Mary laughed heartily. Had she not done so, she would have cried throughout most of her life. Bingo at the French Church (Catholic) was her social life.

These were the people that Elna met most frequently when she ventured out of her flat to procure the needs of her household. Mary O'Malley was to be a lifesaver later on in Elna's life as Mr. Ludins had been in the immediate days following her abandonment by Carl.

On Park Street was an entirely different set of people. Some of those who were part of that landscape were those who lived in apartments above the business establishments which fronted on the sidewalks below them. For many of them the third and fourth floor grill-guarded windows were all the outside space they could claim. Occasionally there was a wave from someone "up there" to someone "down there" - not always clear to onlookers for whom those waves were intended, but waves that called the attention of those below.

Of the people below, Father Cody was a regular as he crossed from the rectory fronting on Park Street to St. Anne's Church which also fronted on Park Street. Charles Thibodeau usually rocked on the first floor porch of 93 Putnam Street, one house removed from Park Street. The Balickis, immigrants from Poland with American-born children, took advantage of pleasant evenings to stroll among the milling shoppers and sightseers to greet people of their acquaintance.

120

Robert Scully, the Hartford police officer assigned to walk the beat in the neighborhood, was a familiar figure. He made his regular contact with police headquarters from a phone which was suspended from a telephone pole at Putnam and Russ Street, but five blocks of Park Street were part of his beat. Elna met him frequently, and from him she always received an Irish greeting and, as time went by, an Irish blessing to be brought home to the children. The firemen at the fire station were as much a fixture as was Officer Scully.

Sixteen-thousand people made up the neighborhood called Frog Hollow and at any given time after 4:30 p.m. when the factories and other businesses closed for the day - three-thousand or more of them used Park Street for one thing or another - with some of them just sight-seeing and breathing that which was considered fresh air even though polluted with all of the ingredients expelled from industrial plants.

Of those thousands, there were those who became Elna's American friends, who like the Danes were hyphenated Americans. With each encounter there was a pleasant exchange of some kind.

Elna was poor! She had little with which to do anything extra. But Elna was rich! A whole world of richness surrounded her and helped her through a difficult time in life.

Transition

The departure of the Andersen brothers and the arrival of George Harding marked a turning point for Elna. The Andersen brothers both left for good reasons. Gustav had fallen in love and was doing well enough to propose marriage to the lady with whom he kept company. The two of them needed a place of their own which it turned out was a third floor, four-room flat, at 12 Troy Street. Oscar had found another job with better hours that suggested a change of address for him. The departure of the Andersens and George Harding's offer to occupy the space vacated by the Andersen brothers created no economic crisis for Elna, but it signified for Elna a change in her business.

For several years those who came to Elna for a place to sleep were Danish and represented a significant stream of young Danish men who had arrived directly from Denmark. They were a part of that stream of immigrants of which Elna, herself, was a part. Now that stream was slowing, and the number of Danish-born applicants for space at her five-room flat had declined. In addition, the Danes who had arrived from Denmark for several decades were now declining in numbers and were becoming "Americanized." It was not quite as important to them that they have a place in a Danish speaking home. What was true for them was also true for Elna. Her openness to renting to non-Danes did not seem as uncomfortable as such a move would have been earlier.

While the arrangement with George Harding was generous, Elna could see the handwriting on the wall about continuing in a business that was dependent on a constant flow of immigrants from Denmark. Until she could set the stage for another source of income, she rented to others who were not of Danish origin. Among those was a man, named Eddie Harris, from Patterson New Jersey - a shoe salesman who often spent days "on the road" selling shoes in wholesale lots to shoe stores dotting the states of Connecticut, Massachusetts and Upper New York. His "roadster" was usually parked on the street, always giving evidence of his residency in one of the apartments - in this case, Elna's five-room flat.

Also helping to fill the void created by new patterns of settlement of Danish immigrant boys was an old bachelor Swede, who indicated that he would like to stay there because of the proximity of 144 to his place of employment - the old Congregational Church on Asylum Street - just over the tracks and away from the factory district in which Elna's place was located. A stipulation to which Elna agreed was that Andy

Hansson - that was his name - could brew his own beer under the kitchen sink. The only requirement on his part was that he exclusively would prepare the brew and that no one was to touch the brew until it was ready for bottling, also a task which he performed.

Again Elna was reluctant - inspite of the fact that she was assured that he would care for all of the details of brewing the beer and that he would not drink too much of it at one time. But Elna agreed, and Andy moved in - in the bed vacated by Eddie Harris.

And so the renters came. And so they went. It was much too unstable a situation for Elna to live with for any length of time.

For some time Elna had been musing about a job at one of the factories nearby - one to which she could walk. In her musing the welfare of her children played a large role. Her children were now six and five years of age and very self sufficient for their age. Maybe she could leave them, if she could arrange to come home for lunch and return to her work station within the span of one hour which the factories allowed for lunch. The concern for her children weighed heavily in her thinking, but so did the need for adequate income - income which had been somewhat erratic for the recent year and one half. Her neighbors? Would there be any among them who could be helpful? Irish, French, German, Italian, Jewish, Polish! Would cultures come into conflict with her concept of what would be needed for two very responsible, but young people?

Elna conferred with Mary O'Malley upstairs. Mary understood Elna's dilemma. She had found herself in the same dilemma in an earlier - though more prosperous - time. Mrs. O'Malley (she was always addressed with this formal title) assured her that she could look after the children who by this time had started school and who would be home alone only very early in the morning and for a short period of time after school. "You just send them up to me!" she declared in her Irish brogue. With her physical limitations from arthritis, Mrs. O'Malley was not able to come down the stairs from her third floor flat very often.

After much soul searching Elna decided she should try to get on at the Merrow Machine Company, a company which manufactured commercial sewing machines and a family company with about 100 employees. She could use her sister and her brother as references. Karna, her sister, still worked there, and Peter, her brother, had worked there and both had been, and were, reliable and good employees. Having spent time studying English, other and better opportunities had presented themselves to Peter, who moved on as soon as he

Elna at thirty-two

thought it was appropriate for him to ask for his release from employment at Merrow's.

Elna's trip to the factory took only about six minutes - one city block west, down a flight of old wooden stairs with exactly one hundred steps, a brief walk over a bridge spanning the Park River and one block past the Underwood Typewriter Company and she was there. She was to see Mr. Washburn, who was in charge of employing new people. A bit nervous, she found Mr. Washburn a very gentle man and a man who was sympathetic to her situation. He shared with her that he would like to hire her, but with her age and with her responsibilities, he could not pay what he was sure she would need to care for her household. "Right now we are employing younger women who can get along on a whole lot less," he said.

124

Elna was crushed! At age 32 - too old? It made no sense to her. She was sure that she could manage. She cried - without tears on the journey past her neighbors, but with big tears upon entering her flat on the second floor at 144 Putnam Street. She did not want her children to be alarmed, but the pain was too great. She had to cry!

Dress making and alterations took on a higher priority than they had in an earlier time. Employment possibilities danced around in her mind in every quiet moment, of which there were some. Critical self evaluations took place. Could she have presented herself better than she had? Everything short of panic filled her breast in spite of assurance from her many friends, both in the neighborhood and at church. Pastor Valdemar Jensen and his wife, Lene, were very comforting in this critical time. Not given to house calling, which Lene saw as her husband's responsibility, Lene wandered around the corner to 144 to give a word of comfort and to bring a little something for the table at mealtime.

Mrs. Back came with containers of newly pasteurized milk and an invitation for Elna to come and bring the children to her home where the children could watch the process of pasteurizing milk and play with the "mousers" that roamed freely in the house and the dairy.

It was a difficult time for Elna - more difficult than the days when she prepared for a lifetime departure from her family to bring her sister Christine to America in 1922.

A Dramatic Decade

Nineteen-thirty-two was not only a year of transition in the source of Elna's support, it was a year of reflection on what had taken place in her life in the decade from 1922 to 1932.

The trip to America was to have been one of brief duration, but it had turned into a decade on American soil filled with excitement, pleasure, apprehension, pain and a deep reliance on her faith and her cultural heritage. It was to have been one of an expeditious delivery of a younger sister to a childless aunt and uncle with an anticipated stay of about six months before returning to Denmark to continue her life there. It turned out to be something else.

Upon disembarking from a Scottish ship in New York, it was a struggle with a language of which she knew nothing. It was a hastily arranged place of employment as a domestic - coupled with leisure hours spent mostly in Perth Amboy, New Jersey, with *Den Danske Ungdomsforening* (The Danish Young People Society). It was a whirl-wind love affair with a handsome young immigrant resulting in a marriage with a very romantic beginning that resulted in two children - one in New Jersey and one in Connecticut. It was a period of excruciating pain when her handsome husband, deserted her in the mid-summer of 1929. It was a period of slow recovery aided by the determination of developing and carrying out a program of self-support. It was a time of sharing with immigrants of other ethnic backgrounds the pain and the struggles of the Great Depression.

The Great Depression was devastating, not only in the United States, but also in Europe and the Far East. With the market collapse on Wall Street in 1929, factories closed, banks closed, merchants closed their shops. Unemployment grew at an astronomical pace. So grim was that period in the world's history that in one year (1931) in the United States alone more than 20,000 people committed suicide. Homeless people slept everywhere and anywhere. They slept under "Hoover Blankets." The streets were awash with people who begged for something to eat. A theme song for the period, even when there was not much to sing about, was "Brother, Can You Spare a Dime?"

Under the circumstances of the decade, Elna survived and became immersed in life in America - struggling with all the others who came for a "better life." The theme song of the period became Elna's theme song, not with mockery of those who were found to be on the streets begging for their very existence, but as an expression of what she

126

considered her good fortune. In spite of everything, she had found her dime. Part of that good fortune was that she had a place to live, and she had her two children who served to give her a special place. Her very modest quarters on the second floor of 144 looked like a palace to her, and those who were fortunate enough to be able to rent from her shared her point of view. Most of the renters had jobs most of the time even if some of those jobs were shared with roommates and others in the area. A half week's pay was better than no pay at all.

Besides comfortable shelter, Elna would often say, "And den I havf my heldt!" And without verbalizing it, Elna would make reference to her rich spiritual heritage which was a blend of her Danish heritage and a living faith - now personified in the person of Pastor Valdemar S. Jensen and other Danish Americans who were also a reflection of both.

With all of the struggle of her first decade in America, 1932 had now dealt her another rejection, as it were, when she failed to gain employment at the Merrow Machine Company.

There was not much time to spend on failures - whether of her own doing or not. Elna's energy needed to be applied to the alternative in which she chose to become engaged. As she labored a glimmer of hope began to permeate the nation that had always held high its concern for the poor and the downtrodden. That glimmer of hope came from a presidential candidate who was making it clear that his leadership was to be a "New Deal" for the "Forgotten Man." That glimmer of hope captured the imagination of the people who lived in Frog Hollow, the inner city ghetto of which 144 was a part.

As Elna mused about Franklin Delano Roosevelt's rhetoric, Elna realized that she was immersed in American democracy - a democracy to which she had not given much thought. When you are Danish, you are Danish. But now! Now, she was becoming an American. That very discovery caused her to look toward citizenship in a land that seemed destined to be the one in which she would find new meaning for her life. "Efter all," she would say, "my children are Americans."

With what little time that was available to her, Elna sought out, with the help of her pastor and her neighbors, the office from which she could get reading material and application papers for citizenship. The late evening hours were spent reading (in English) the instructions for becoming a part of the economically awaking giant among the nations of the earth.

On April 18, 1932, in the U.S. District Court in Hartford, Connecticut, with her two children and in the presence of the many others who were also seeking citizenship, Elna took the oath of loyalty to the United States of America, with C.E. Pickett, the Clerk of Court, giving record of that fact.

For much of the decade that preceded her application for citizenship, Elna had looked with a good deal of nostalgia to Denmark with the dream that one day she might return there, but the events of the decade had eroded that dream, and now the promises of a better day in America had convinced her that America would be her new home.

The
American Elna

The American Elna

Elna was proud to be an American. And, now, she was a "documented" American. If her pride in her new country did not show, she had a piece of paper that would remove all doubt.

Apart from the little piece of paper that said she was now an American citizen, there was little else that made that fact clear. She owned no property, except for "the immigrant bed collection" on which her renters rested their tired bodies. (The "immigrant bed collection" was just that. Most of the beds were of the brass head and foot variety - in very bad condition.) An old black kitchen stove had come with her when she and Carl moved from Grandview Terrace to 144 Putnam Street. A wobbly old oak table and three wiggly chairs - two of oak and one of birch - also came from Grandview Terrace. The remainder of her possessions consisted mostly of a few cooking and eating utensils and the clothes on her back. Nothing that she owned said "American" - though one of the brass beds was stamped with a label that said "Bridgeport Brass Works"- obviously from Bridgeport, Connecticut.

Elna paid no taxes, so there were no tax receipts. She received no government aid or assistance, the receipts of which would have included a notation about her status in America. She had no sales receipts, since most of her belongings came as cash transactions with people who had owned the items in an earlier time.

Elna's language betrayed any indication that she might be American. She just could not master some of the American words without giving away the fact that she had come from Europe. "Kitzen" was one of those words that she just could not say. And phrases like "ud paa porchen," "hen til Park Street," "ned til churchen" made it very clear that Elna was still a Dane, or from some other European country.

Elna was a hyphenated American, a concept that she never questioned, but her "papers" did not say that. They said that she was now an American, and she was proud of that fact.

Even as Elna prepared for citizenship on that April day in 1932, she had been thinking about "divorce" - a word that was high up on her list of words of profanity. Elna had been advised that the little that she had could be claimed by Carl should he ever return and that she should protect herself against that eventuality. Before becoming a citizen she wasn't entirely sure that a court would rule in her favor, but somehow in her mind her new status in America assured her that she would not lose the little that she had.

Again, with the assistance of her pastor and newfound church friends, Elna proceeded to the Hartford County Courthouse to the Office of Judge Baldwin to fill out the papers which were required. Under the reason for the divorce, Elna had listed "desertion" - a word that she had on a little piece of paper that she held. In the place where the date of the desertion was to be written, she entered - June 10, 1929. The remaining information simply declared who she knew herself to be, and, importantly, in the place where she was to write "citizenship" she proudly wrote, "American."

It was a painful day - June 16, 1933 - which once again brought fleetingly to her mind the thought that she had entertained from time to time during Carl's four-year absence that "Carl would come to himself and come home again." Once again the thought had to be dismissed, and with the same bravado that she had displayed throughout her life, she descended the courthouse steps back into the "real" world of living her life for, and with, her two children and the many friends that she had accumulated throughout her journey in America.

As Elna proceeded with matters that she had never thought she would entertain, the world around her was changing. The moods of people were changing - especially for the masses who struggled for their existence for one reason or another in depressed America. A new president had made promises, and now he was in the White House as the nation's leader. Here and there a company which had guarded its cash was now willing to take on new employees. Mobility of families increased as those families moved to where the jobs were.

The young men who lived with Elna were no exception to the increased mobility. Most of them settled up with Elna before they departed for greener pastures, but a few left Elna with their IOUs. With an increasingly erratic pattern of renting beds to single males, Elna found herself in need of some of the money which was owing to her. And with that need, came a new pursuit - "Collection of Unpaid Rent."

Some of Elna's energetic pursuit paid off, but from time to time there were those who did not make good on their IOUs. It was a serious disappointment for Elna who had always believed that the integrity of Danes was without blemish. Some gave the excuse that hard times were still upon them and that they would pay when that changed. Others left the addresses which Elna had - with no forwarding address.

Inspite of the continuing stress on Elna's survival plan, other "Avon Lady" programs held little appeal. Having all but given up on Avon, Elna looked at Watkins Products and other household and beauty products. An occasional sale filled the blank spaces left by unpaid rent. And budget tightening became ever more important - just at a time when the whole nation was awakening to a new environment of optimism under the "New Deal."

As the year 1933 approached its last day and as Elna struggled with her various activities trying to make a living, she mused often about the Merrow Machine Company - the company from which she had been turned away the year before. "Could it be that this company has discovered a need for new employees and would they be willing to talk with her again?" Elna mused. In a moment of renewed energy, Elna set out - west one block on Mortson Street to Pope Park where the flight of one hundred stairs was, over the bridge spanning the Park River and past the Underwood Typewriter Company to Mr. Washburn's office.

Elna spent a long time with Mr. Washburn, finally convincing him that she could handle the most menial work at the sewing machine factory - certainly with the thought of some promotions, if she proved herself. Mr. Washburn eventually decided that he would take on no undue risk in employing Elna who agreed to the starting wage of $.35 an hour - $14.00 a week. She was to start on Monday, January 8th at 7:00 a.m. with one hour off for lunch at noon and resuming her duties at 1:00 p.m. to 4:00 p.m. Someone would be there to get her started.

Living by the Clock

The factory job at the Merrow Machine Company brought great changes in the lifestyle of Elna and her children. Prior to Elna's employment at Merrow's her life-style could be described as necessarily flexible - adjusting to the variety of tasks that she engaged in to generate income for the family. Now life was lived almost exclusively by the clock.

Factory hours at Merrow Machine Company were from 7:00 a.m. to 12:00 noon with resumption of work beginning at 1:00 p.m., continuing on to 4:00 p.m., the normal hours for factory work in the neighborhood and throughout the city of Hartford, for that matter. Beginning as early as 6:00 a.m. the streets teamed with people headed off to the manufacturing jobs that produced all kinds of machinery to facilitate life in a relatively new nation among nations of the world. Buses and trolley cars, which throughout the day ran at fifteen-minute intervals, moved about the city at five-minute intervals until most people were at their factory stations - usually five minutes before production was to begin. For Elna that meant departure from 144 by 6:45 a.m. to be on time at Merrow's.

With school children at home, Elna's work obviously began much earlier than the 6:45 a.m. departure time. There was her own grooming and homemaker chores that needed to be cared for as well as breakfast preparations for her children, so that they could be off to school. To get the work done Elna responded to an alarm clock at 5:30 a.m. every morning. By her departure time, school clothing had been laid out, a breakfast table set - often with a last minute instruction noted on a pad which lay at the center of the breakfast table.

For several weeks before beginning her new job Elna had prepared for her morning duties and for those duties which were to be that of her children during her absence from the home. All of it began with regular chats about the new style of life that was to be "out there" for all the members of the family. Included as part of those chats for everyone was great emphasis on "timeliness." To make vivid that emphasis, her two children were each given a "brand new" Westclock alarm clock. Instructions were given on how to wind the clock and how to set it for both time and alarm. There was a review of where things needed for finalizing breakfast preparation could be found and where those items were to be returned upon the completion of the morning meal. Little, if anything, was said in instructing her two children about getting along with each other in the absence of their mother. It was simply expected that there would be no problem in that regard. The instructions were regularly concluded with the observation that should there be any problems, Mrs. O'Malley, who lived upstairs, could be consulted.

As a final part of the preparation, Elna provided each of her children with a key to the second floor flat with the instruction that none of the children of the neighborhood or from school classes were to be in the apartment in their mother's absence. The last admonition was to guard carefully that key which would give them admission to "safe" ground.

If there was any apprehension about the new arrangements, it was not evident in Elna. There were minimal trial runs in the few days that preceded the new style of life, but other than that, it was expected that all would do their part as required.

After the new program for living was begun, late afternoon and evenings were especially precious as each member of the household shared something of the day as it had been lived at the factory, the school and during the journeys to and from factory and school. School recess times received a lot of attention. There was some sense of community in being a part of the city of Hartford designated as Frog Hollow. Children from the neighborhood did not always play by the same rules. And it soon become evident that the "play" at the factory and on the street between work and home did not always go by the same ground rules either. There was much to talk about in the "wider" world of which the Olsen family, for the most part, got only glimpses with their earlier homebound lifestyle.

But with all of the variations of the new lifestyle, scheduling of activities of importance for the family became easier. The hours at the factory and the school, provided windows of freedom which could be counted on. Along with those windows of freedom now was regular income which could be budgeted with the same precision that the hours of the day could be designated. For the first time since the birth of Elna's first child there was a little "extra" to "do with," and events, especially those of a cultural nature, could be included in the calendar of activity.

With less than a mile to the city center, a host of possibilities for learning and entertainment came into view. Weekend stage shows at the State Theater, featuring bands of the big band era, provided an occasional treat. Sound movie theaters were an attraction, and a great improvement over the silent movies which were rapidly giving way to electronic development. The Hartford Public Library, later to be headed by a Dane from the Holstebro area of Jylland, Denmark (Elna's childhood playground), was within easy walking distance.

134

The Horace Bushnell Memorial Hall stood in the shadows of the Connecticut State Capitol only a few blocks from 144 - a hall in which major dramas of the world were played with international talent. Political rallies were held on the State Capitol grounds - attended by thousands of blue collar workers who hoped always to hear of a better day.

G. Fox & Co., Browne-Thompson, Sage & Allen, Sears Roebuck and Co. together with Kresge's Department Store and Marholin's Hardware Company and other significant stores carrying the latest of everything punctuated Main Street - and now there was money to "go and look at," if not to buy, that which was available. Saturday, a day off from factory duties, brought in thousands of shoppers from all of central Connecticut.

Sunday remained a special day. Our Savior's Lutheran Church, as always, had been a part of Elna's Hartford life and remained so even after the change of their weekday life. The definite schedule that accompanied her employment did not alter the importance of Sunday as a day of worship, but the change did preclude some activity held at Our Savior's Church during the week. While Elna had not participated on a regular basis in the Ladies Aid (*Kvindeforeningen*) meetings of Our Savior's Lutheran Church, it was now plain that she would be excluded by her new schedule from attending any of those meetings. On the other hand, there were in addition to Sunday morning worship, activities in which fellow Danes could participate which coincided with the schedules of others in the greater Hartford area who also lived their lives by the clock. These activities found their place among the many options which were now becoming available to Elna.

Domination by the clock created some limitations to be sure, but it also opened all kinds of opportunities for enrichment and living - both of which Elna enjoyed.

Factory and Other Friends

Elna's employment at The Merrow Machine Company brought her into contact with a new neighborhood - a neighborhood which up until now had not been evident to her. Until 1934 Elna's neighborhood consisted mostly of the people who lived in the same building, a few people who were free during the day to shop on Park Street, and the members of Our Savior's Danish Lutheran Church, who - mostly on Sundays - paid her a visit at 144. Being preoccupied with operating a rooming house and caring for her children, Elna had not consciously become aware of the large numbers of people who moved about the neighborhood in the early hours of the morning and again in the late hours of the afternoon. These people were her neighbors - the neighbors she rarely saw, but who clearly were part of the mix.

Elna's employment at Merrow's made her a part of that large group of people whose factory employment dictated that they be on the street at - what for some were - ungodly hours in the morning.

On Mortson Street alone - a short city block which ran between Putnam Street and Park Terrace - there were 500 people, approximately 100 of whom were employed by Underwood Typewriter Co., Spencer Turbine, Hartford Machine Screw Company, and Arrow, Hart and Heggeman - companies which grew up along the New York, New Haven and Hartford Railroad and the Park River which emptied into the Connecticut River a little over one mile distant. Still others came from apartment buildings of a similar nature to those on Mortson Street from Putnam Heights, Park Street, York Street and Ward Street. For five days out of each week, Elna was a part of that mix.

It became clear after several weeks of participating with that group that there was a group of people who was always a part of the same flow that Elna took to work and another group who were always a part of the journey home.

Among those who became a regular companion on each of the five workdays was Andrea Anderson - a lady with Swedish roots whose husband had immigrated from Sweden. The subject for conversation, which usually was initiated by Andy, centered around a husband who was less than understanding about most things and "investing in the market" - the local over-the-counter market and the New York Market. It mattered little to Andy that Elna no longer had a husband and that there was little in the way of financial resources to consider investing in anything. Andy, with ritual regularity, used the twelve minutes to and from work each day to give each of the subjects exhaustive treatment. Andy had lost a "bundle" in the collapse of the market in 1929, but investing was in her blood.

Occasionally Andy was not present for reasons not always made known to Elna, and on many of those occasions Elna was joined by Charles Gastineau - a tall, stately man - who slowed the pace for Elna who quickly gained the label "trotter" by the ladies who, in fair weather, awaited their spouses in the afternoon. Among those women who usually sat on the front porch of 18 Mortson Street were Maureen Tibideaux, Julia Swahn and Charlie's wife, Therese. Charles and Therese had three children - William, Louise and Maurice and conversation very quickly turned to raising children in a neighborhood where moral and religious standards varied dramatically. The Gastineaus were Roman Catholic and Charles was an even-keeled man. His general outlook on life was calm and considered, never panicky. He was a good one to share common concerns about family life - both religious and otherwise - in the Frog Hollow neighborhood.

Magnus Martinsen, a fellow Dane, who was not a part of the immediate neighborhood, often passed by the intersection of Putnam and Mortson Streets as Elna approached her home. Occasionally there were opportunities to exchange a bit about the Danish community which was not related to the church, except by ethnicity and mutual friends "who spent more time at church den dey neededt to" in Martinsen's judgement.

Marian O'Toole often stepped from the Connecticut Company bus just in time to exchange a few words with Elna about things in the inner city. Marian worked for Traveler's Insurance Company in the underwriting department and lived next door to Elna. She was never visible at 6:45 in the morning, but frequently was there at quitting time. Marian had cared for her mother in an earlier time and now kept house for her brother Bill, who was relatively unknown in the neighborhood, but had gained a reputation because he owned an automobile - one which was rarely driven, but which was always polished to showroom specifications.

A feature of Elna's daily route was a journey through Pope Park which included the stairway of exactly 100 steps from Park Terrace down to the Park River where the bridge connected the residential section of Frog Hollow with the industrial buildings that fronted on the river's west bank. Because Elna made it a point to be home at the noon hour to provide lunch for her children, this stairway became a twice daily part of her routine. On most days the stairway provided all of the exercise that a busy young mother needed to stay healthy. For Elna's children it was a fascination to know that "Mom did it again" as part of her work routine.

The school clock demanded a different schedule for Elna's children than the clock established for Elna. Both Harold and Alice were home from school earlier in the day than was the case for Elna. With something always to share from the day's "work" at school, both the children soon adopted a program of meeting their mother at the foot of the park stairs so they could participate in the exercise and challenge of their Mom's quick ascent of that long stairway.

When Elna shared the story of her journey to and from work, she always added that among her companions and friends were her two children - if not always in person, then in thought.

Planning for Visitors from Denmark

Spring blossomed in Pope Park adding to the joy that Elna experienced going to and from the Merrow Machine Company. With the spring blossoms came a wonderful perfume which blunted the scent of machine oil which was always a part of the day at the factory. Elna drank deeply of nature's aromas which wafted through the air - especially in the early hours of the day.

But there was more than spring in the air in early April of 1934. There was an anticipatory joy brought on by plans of the immigrant Laumark children to bring their parents to the United States of America. Of the nine Carl Jespersen children, seven had emigrated from Denmark to find a new and more prosperous life. With Elna's employment at Merrow's, all of the Jespersen Laumarks who had come to America were settled and had "good jobs." They could now give thought to bringing their parents to see how well it was going for them.

Viggo, the eldest son of Carl Jespersen and next in line after Elna, had settled in South River, New Jersey. Not far from South River, Viggo had also found employment with an Italian-American who ran a construction company, building highways for the growing number of Americans who now could afford automobiles - automobiles which took them to their places of employment and the recreational areas of New York and New Jersey. In his free time Viggo had met a fun-loving German girl from Koblenz, who like the young immigrants of Denmark, had come to the United States for a more prosperous life. Marie Trimborn had been discovered by Viggo at the community pub where the "poor and tired" gathered for refreshment after long weeks at hard work. Vig and Marie married in 1929 and by mid 1934 had two children.

Karna, Carl Jespersen's fourth child, had come to the United States in early 1926, settling in Hartford, Connecticut where she found employment at the Merrow Machine Company later that year. Karna's social life was lived mostly at the Danish Brotherhood Hall on White Street where she met Chris Carstensen, "a handsome young man with a disarming smile." Married in 1929, Karna and Chris had no children but by 1934 were nicely settled in a bit more up-scale apartment, just below Trinity College on Ward Place in Hartford.

Christine, who had found a suitor in Anton Nielsen - a man several years her senior - lived in Metuchen, New Jersey, on Bissett Place, just behind the Main Street Motion Picture Theater. It was a nice neighborhood and was convenient for Anton in getting to and from his work as a brick mason of some reputation. Married in late 1929 on the same day that Karna and Chris had married, Anton and Christine were now parents of a bright two year old son who kept the household entertained with his energy and his curiosity about everything.

Martin, Peter and Ejner Christian completed the group of seven Jespersen Laumark children who followed their older siblings to the metropolitan New York area for a richer life. Martin had joined his brother, Viggo, in highway construction. Peter got on at Merrow's in Hartford and was renting a room from Elna. Ejner Christian landed an apprenticeship with a painting contractor in the Perth Amboy area of New Jersey.

The seven children, through the mail and a phone call where possible - laid plans for gathering up money for passage for Carl and Jensine Jespersen of Hanbjerg, Denmark, and arranging for their appropriate visiting while in the United States. With limited free time and limited communication facilities, it was the spring of 1936 before the U.S.A. Laumark contingent was able to get the package put together. July and August were the planned months for the roundtrip ocean voyage.

Arranging for financing and a more specific date for a visit from their parents, as it turned out, was the least of the difficulties associated with the visit to the United States. The greater difficulty occurred when the seven children plus the two households of an earlier generation that had emigrated to America, sought to develop an itinerary for "equal time" for all of the households concerned. It did not take long to determine that a base should be established in New Jersey where four of the Jespersen Laumark families had settled and where Jensine's brother, Peder, and her sister, Karen, had established homes many years earlier.

In making that decision the Connecticut Jespersen Laumarks also had to be considered. In two of the households language did not need to be considered. Both Karna and Chris Carstensen spoke Danish, of course, with English that clearly indicated that they were from a foreign country. Elna's children spoke fluent Danish but at ages ten and eight, respectively, were not able to "take charge" of grandparents who would be left with them much of the time while Elna pursued her responsibilities at the Merrow Machine Company. Peter had married, but married a true "Connecticut Yankee" whose family could trace its ancestry to the early English families who settled in Puritan America. Clearly the planning was not simple.

140

With the vist of parents still approximately two years distant there was some time to arrange an itinerary for the Jespersens and to arrange a base in each of the two areas of Danish settlement of the early twentieth century. Ultimately it was determined that Carl and Jensine should "live" with the Anton Nielsens in Metuchen, New Jersey, and in Connecticut with Karna and Chris Carstensen. Both residences had, or could create, a vacant bedroom. Both families had automobiles. Both families had telephones. Both households had a Jespersen Laumark daughter who did not have to appear at a factory or other place of employment.

When the summer of 1936 arrived, Carl and Jensine Jespersen, with the help of their Denmark children, set out for Copenhagen and for their six-day ocean voyage to New York. The sailing was not as relaxing as it had been for Elna and Christine who noted repeatedly that the Atlantic had been like "glass" all the way. Carl disembarked in New York, obviously very stressed from the journey and for several days walked as though he were still onboard a rocking and swaying ship. Jensine, whose disposition was generally more calm, said little except that she was glad to be on dry land again and in the company of her family in the new land.

It would be several days after Carl and Jensine arrived in New York before the two of them felt they had strength enough to begin a vigorous program of visiting everybody in America. While they rested, they wondered about all of those they had not yet seen. Would they be well? Would they have adequate means to have a wholesome life? Though it seemed to be self-evident, the question of permanent residency in America arose within the parental couple. It would be so nice to have them back in Denmark where visits could be more frequent and without the stress that they had just endured.

A "Once in a Lifetime" Family Reunion

Carl and Jensine's visit had begun with their stepping off the ship in New York and continued for the first few days in the home of Christine and Anton Nielsen. Ejner Christian could not wait for a formal invitation to come to see his parents. "Kisse," as his mother affectionately called him, was not married and had no family obligations to which he had to attend. The quiet of his apartment did little to persuade him that he needed to give his father and mother a few moments of rest from the long journey from Holstebro (His father and mother had moved several times since living at Hanbjerg on the family farm). It was as if the aromas of Christine's spectacular culinary preparations penetrated the entire Essex County area, inviting Kisse without the formality of a phone call.

It was not long after the initial days that members of the New Jersey family were invited to come to the Anton Nielsen home. On the first available weekend Viggo and his family were invited to spend Saturday in Metuchen with his father and mother. With them for the visit were Viggo's children, Viggo and Marie (called Sonny and Sis to distinguish them from their parents for whom they had been named). The visiting proceeded with long pauses. Though Christine and Viggo were sister and brother, the two families did not get together often by reason of distance, community involvement and family ties with Marie's family.

Martin, who rented a room from Viggo and Marie in South River, was not able to be along for this first visit. Last among the employed of the construction company for which he worked, it became his turn to work - a work from which there was no reprieve in spite of the significance of the meeting to which he had also been invited

Days of quiet, which both Carl and Jensine had experienced in the initial days in America, became rare. To deal with that Carl took to walking the streets of Metuchen, venturing into the center of the community. He could not help noting that the village seemed to have little pride where neatness and cleanliness were concerned. He compared what he saw with what he knew of his own community in Denmark. He was pleased that his children were doing as well as they were but appalled that they had to live in such unsanitary and unsightly conditions. Jensine rocked each day with knitting needles in hand, every now and then giving expression to her joy at being with her children.

Soon the time came for Carl and Jensine to visit the family in Connecticut. Arrangements were made for Karna and Chris to drive to New Jersey to meet her parents and to transport them to Connecticut. It was a ten and one half hour drive when everything went just right, even in Chris' new Plymouth, though the distance was only 128 miles. The journey required rising at an early hour to get through New York City between the rush hours of the morning and noon.

The first leg of the journey - 23 miles to New Haven - went fairly well. The Berlin Turnpike did not have the traffic that would later be encountered on US Route 1. Unlike US Route 1, it did not go through the center of each town along the way. Route 1, on the other hand, was for the most part a cobbled-stoned roadway - known as the Boston Post Road - going through the center of every southern Connecticut coastal town with a minimum of three traffic lights per community. On most occasions, it seemed, dense fog also hindered travel. Then, in New York, the question arose for the infrequent travelers about necessary turns to be on the right road - the right road being the one that would take them to the Holland Tunnel under the Hudson River and then to make the appropriate turn that would keep them on US Route 1 in New Jersey which skirted Metuchen at its northeast city limits.

Karna and Chris arrived hungry and exhausted at the Anton Nielsen home - not ready to make the return trip very soon.

Visiting became animated upon Karna and Chris' arrival - the first half hour of which was dominated by the difficulties of travel in these United States. Then, came the catch up on what had transpired in New Jersey in the early days of the Danish visitors and at last something about how life had been in Denmark since the departure of the seven Laumark offspring for the "promised" land. And lastly the conversation turned to the stated reason for the Carstensen trip to New Jersey - the transfer of the parents to Connecticut for a visit with family there. At the same time there was discussion of how and when to assemble the entire family in one place for a complete family reunion of those who probably would never have an opportunity to be a part of that experience again. A long weekend disappeared and soon the journey to Connecticut was to begin.

Carl Jespersen became impatient with the time involved in making the trip to New England. Jensine sat quietly musing about discoveries that would be theirs in the much larger city of Hartford - larger than Metuchen. The children who wrote home (Karna and Christine, primarily) had often indicated in their letters that Elna, the eldest, lived on the edge of poverty and that many of her days had been very difficult in the new land - especially after her abandonment by Carl. Jensine's quiet thoughts pondered those reports with some apprehension about what she might see upon her arrival at Elna's place.

So great was the joy for Jensine when she saw Elna's flat at 144 that she could not help exclaim about how wonderful things looked. Elna's home was neat and clean, her children reflected a joy at being a part of the home, and the pantry did seem to have enough food to feed the family, including the visitors from Europe. There were few signs of the poverty which had been reported. In the quiet of the evening Jensine sat back in a barrel-backed chair and sighed a sigh of joy and thanksgiving. *"O Gud, du ska' ha' tak!"*

The days in Connecticut fled past and soon all were on their way to New Jersey, including Peter and his wife, Florence, to participate in the family reunion about which conversation had been held prior to the Connecticut trip. It was to be held at *Moster* Karen and Uncle Rudolf's home on Woodbridge Drive in South River. Rudolf's garden served as the arena for revelling and exchange and included Rudolf and Karen's son Frank and his wife Mae and their two children, Donald and Elaine, together with Karen and Jensine's brother Peter and his wife, Marie, who lived not far away in Sayreville. A neighbor was enlisted to catch the gathering on a Kodak Brownie camera - a picture that captured the "once in a life time" family reunion for the Jespersen Laumark family.

144

Fit for a Fiddle

The factory hours and the flight of one-hundred steps through Pope Park provided many things, not least "regularity" and "exercise" - two ingredients for good health. Both ingredients served Elna well as she addressed her mental health. They made her "fit for a fiddle." And that fiddle belonged to Niels Lund, a Danish immigrant, who became a part of the Hartford Symphony Orchestra - a group in which he occupied first chair as violinist.

Niels was well versed in a variety of cultures to which he had been exposed through his participation in symphony orchestras in both Denmark and America. He liked the variety and style of the music and often read up on the cultures from which the music emanated. Inspite of that exposure, deep in his soul was the music of his native land and, more particularly, the music of the peasant people out of whom he had come.

When Niels reached for his fiddle at gatherings of Danes in the metro-Hartford area, most Danes took on the rhythm of the music played for a variety of folk dances, some of which were universally Danish and others definitely parochial. It was not long before a group of Danes, and in some cases their children, gathered as regulars for sessions of Danish folk dancing.

An interesting variety of people assembled to this call. Among them was A.C. Petersen, one of central Connecticut's leading dairymen. "A.C." had developed in a few short years a thriving business in pasteurizing milk from his countrymen who had become dairy farmers and from others in the area who had dairy herds. A.C. was a pioneer in the Ice Cream Parlor business, and A.C.'s ice cream store became a part of the vocabulary of all the European immigrant groups that settled in the Hartford area of industrial Connecticut.

A competitor, and a good friend, was Emil Godiksen who, with Martin Arends, established the Lincoln Dairy - also in the business of pasteurizing and delivering milk to the various neighborhoods throughout the metro Hartford area. One step ahead of A.C. in some things, Emil established a number of neighborhood dairy stores at which the citizenry of central Connecticut could gather for an ice cream cone on hot humid nights.

These two men, together with their wives - Anna and Eleanor, respectively - were not only vitally engaged in the dancing activity, they often provided a green pasture alongside a dairy barn where the

145

dancers could dance until their hearts were content and their feet hurt.

Benny Melberg, a machinist foreman for Pratt & Whitney Aircraft, took his place among the dancers, together with his wife, Louise. Benny together with the Petersens and the Godiksens and still another couple, Kris and Karen Hemme, formed only one of the squares for folk dancing of which there could sometimes be as many as four.

Elna came not as part of a couple. Like Niels' wife, Aase, she had to find a partner among the "dancing Danes," but there was little difficulty in finding a partner. The young Olesen boys, Jetter and Jesper, were more than willing to serve as partners for a number of ladies who needed dancing partners. Karen Lauridsen Smith was willing to share her non-Danish husband, Ed, so that the single ladies present could be part of the music and clapping and swinging and singing which were all a part of the wonderful outings in and around Hartford.

Jacob and Bertine Norregaard, who had made their way to Hartford by way of Minneapolis, were also part of the group and brought new steps and formations to the lively gatherings that left the participants, exhausted but filled with a renewed spirit of who they had come to know themselves to be. "It was a good tired," Elna would often say after having spent a day on the "green dance floor" of a farmstead, owned and operated by an immigrant Dane.

In a very real sense the dancing did not stop with the departure from the dance floor. Danish hymns and songs and dance tunes continued for hours, sometimes days, in the minds of the participants in the folk dancing. It was music that sustained them in the multicultural setting in which they found themselves in their work. For Elna it was important to have the identity that the folk dancing group provided. The lingering music gave strength to her soul and guidance for her life.

The music brought life to the menial activity of the production line of the Merrow Machine Company. There was a pride, of course, in producing the finest sewing machine needles for commercial use, but it could be devastatingly demeaning, regardless of which position on the assembly line of production one occupied. (There were twenty-eight such positions - all of which Elna occupied throughout the thirty-four years of employment in the "high speed, over seam" sewing machine factory.)

The activity of these adult Danes, which included Elna, generated interest in a similar group for the young people - "kidsener" as they were called. It was not long before a regular group of thirty to forty young people gathered to drink of an enriching heritage. New names in the

146

The Nels Lund Folk Dancers
(Elna is second from left)

The Nels Lund Folk Dancers enjoy green dance floor
at the A.C. Petersen farm.

children's group made it clear that the older folks were not only able to nurse their own souls, but their influence was to pass on to a new generation. It was not always clear to all of the older generation that a full preservation of the Danish culture would not be possible, but what was to become clear was that the young generation was interested in a heritage - a heritage which fused a faith and culture which had been imported from Denmark.

The musicians for the younger group were made up of a number of people. Among them was Willie Melberg, the younger son of Benny and Lousie Melberg, who had learned to play the violin and who had learned the rhythm of the Danish folk dances. The young people learned not only the music and the dance steps, but they learned that costuming was also important. Both the boys and the girls, when it came to exhibition time, were dressed with costumes that reflected the traditional dress of various locations in Denmark.

The young people from as far away as Manchester, Bloomfield, and Bristol, Connecticut, were sufficiently regular to indicate the importance of this activity in rearing young Danes in a new land. Florence Salmonsen from Manchester rarely missed. Eigel Larsen from Farmington was among the regulars as were his sisters, Vivian and Wanda. Elna's two children, Harold and Alice, could walk to dance sessions and rarely missed a gathering.

Elna was "fit for a fiddle" but many others shared the same fitness that made for people of integrity and balance , ready to contribute to the fabric of a developing new land which was already well-known throughout the world as "the melting pot" of cultures.

Our Savior's Church Struggles with Change

In its nearly fifty years of existence Our Savior's Danish Lutheran Church (chartered on May 31, 1891) had served as a pillar of strength for hundreds of Danish immigrants who had settled in central Connecticut. It also served well a generation of young people born to those immigrants, who were in some ways more Danish than American. Not all who benefitted from the worshipping group known as "the Danish Church" suffered the same kind of trial that had been Elna's during the late twenties and the early thirties, but many found the Danish Church to be a source of strength for them in the various trials which were theirs as newcomers to the western hemisphere.

The young men who came to Elna's for "a nice clean place to stay" were among those who found help at Our Savior's Danish Lutheran Church. Others found job connections and/or assistance in developing their own business at the church located at the corner of Russ and Babcock Streets. In the years that Pastor and Mrs. Valdemar Jensen served the congregation quite a number found financial assistance, if not directly, then by direction to those who were in a position to help.

In spite of its maturity as a Christian congregation, Our Savior's Danish Lutheran Church found itself in need of direction and counsel. The congregation was struggling with a changing constituency. No longer was the congregation exclusively Danish. Not all of the children who were born to immigrant parents felt that they were more Danish than American. Most of them, in fact, had been caught up in the melting pot process of being "Americanized" and were not particularly caught up in loyalties to institutions that did not reflect their feelings or commitments. In a case or two there was a person who had no connection with Denmark who found comfort among the people of the congregation though they were not familiar with the idiom in which the comfort was expressed.

Increasingly the congregation found itself discussing its destiny at congregational meetings - sometimes with fist shaking and almost always with loud voices in the belief that the increased volume would make up for any deficiency of reason which arose out of sheer emotional argument.

"I tink vi shouldt havf Engless evry Sunday," was the cry of some. "Dis iss a Daniss Churtch!" came the retort from the otherside of the *undersal* (basement) where spiritual restraint often gave way to some very worldly language and illustration. "Vel, if vi don't haf Daniss, den

I don't needt to drive twenty-five miles to go to churtch here," came the comment of someone who lived in Wallingford, "andt det er a lot closzer to Bridgeport den it iss her," threatening those who favored some kind of transition to English.

Caught in the middle of the tension which often registered high on the emotional barometer was Pastor V.S. Jensen, who now had been pastor of Our Savior's Church for almost a decade. More than he knew at the time, he became part of the problem because of his rearing in the mid-western Danish-American communities. American born, "V.S." - as he was called by many - was among the American-born Danes who reveled in a fairly well preserved heritage from Denmark. Because that heritage was precious to Pastor Jensen, he found himself on the side of preserving the Danish, while others at the congregational gatherings who were eager to shed their foreign identity spoke vigorously in Danish dialect for English services. "Efter all dis is Amerika! And vi must be Amerikans! Vi needt to learn da language and it shoudt be from the heart."

Also caught in the tension was Elna. Now it was her time to contribute to the life of the congregation in a way that had not been possible for many years due to her family circumstance. In her very gentle way she often rose at meetings of the congregation to declare that "her children ver Americans and dey shouldt have their fate in their hearts as well as their heads." For the first time in her life Elna found herself on the opposite side of the pastor - and in this case one who had helped her a great deal through her earlier struggle. Elna had always looked up to her pastors, but in this matter she strongly believed that the pastor was wrong.

What made it particularly difficult for Elna was that her two children were currently in a confirmation class conducted in Danish by the pastor who insisted on memorization of hymns (some very long) by N.F.S. Grundtvig, Thomas Kingo and Hans Brorson, all of whom had shaped Elna's life dramatically in Denmark in the early years of the twentieth century. With a good deal of strength for her argument was the observation that three out of the eight children in that class could only phonetically mouth the words of the hymns without understanding them because they were fourth generation Scandinavians in the U.S.A.

All kinds of crosscurrents tore at Elna's heart. It was a difficult time for her. "Cut off," was her feeling. Cut off from the source of her strength in those very difficult days in 1929 and the years following when she was left to make it on her own in a "foreign" land.

150

Our Savior's Lutheran Church, like its members, was caught in the crosscurrents - not of theological making, but of sociological change. The struggle became even more intense, when in the midst of the struggle, Pastor Jensen resigned to return to a Midwest congregation in the heart of Audubon County, Iowa, where Danish-American congregations were the rule and not the exception.

Pastors from Bridgeport, Connecticut; Portland, Maine; Troy, New York; and the Bronx in New York City did their best to serve a congregation in tension over language, but also about the larger question of how they might best serve a community which was dwindling in Danish population and radically changing. It became clear from the discussions of the most interested members of the congregation that some new direction was necessary.

As the congregation discussed its future - now dimmed not only by internal struggle, but by dwindling immigration and the determination of new immigrants to identify with the new culture - a pall of discouragement descended upon just about every discussion concerning the congregation's future.

The despair, if it could be described as despair, was short-lived. In the summer of 1938, Pastor Johannes V. Knudsen of Bethlehem Lutheran Church in Askov, Minnesota, answered the call to serve the Hartford congregation. A condition of that call was that Pastor Knudsen be allowed to pursue a doctor's degree at the Hartford Theological Seminary. The classroom study and the interchange with pastors of American churches served to enrich the work of the new pastor at Our Savior's Church. Danish services could continue, but the move to English services became evident with the scheduled times for the English and Danish worship services, the change of confirmation instruction from Danish to English and important exchanges with nearby congregations which were neither Danish nor Lutheran.

The next years were a God-send to Our Savior's Danish Lutheran Church in one of the oldest cities of the United States. Though only fifty years old the congregation became a vital part of a city that was three-hundred years old and an important congregation in the life of new Americans - some born in Denmark and some born on the North American continent of Danish parents.

**Elna Dressed up for
Dining with Danish Royalty**

Dining with Danish Royalty

In taking her strong stand for the use of English in the church services and educational programs of Our Savior's Danish Lutheran Church in America, Elna was still very much a Dane. Memories of Denmark and that country's customs danced regularly in her soul.

At no time was the fact that she was a Danish American more evident than when she, along with other Hartford Danes, was invited to a banquet in honor of their Royal Highnesses, the Crown Prince and Princess of Denmark and Iceland, at the Waldorf Astoria in New York on May 3, 1939. The banquet sponsors were the Danish National Committee for Participation in the New York World's Fair 1939 and the American Denmark Committee.

Several thousand invitations were sent to people in both Denmark and the United States in anticipation of a gathering worthy of the visit of Crown Prince Frederik and Crown Princess Ingrid. The banquet hall at the Waldorf Astoria was huge and provided for one-thousand guests with ten to a table. Among the guests were Professor Niels Bohr, the world famous atomic scientist of Denmark; opera singer Lauritz Melchior also of Denmark and from America two pastors of the Danish Evangelical Lutheran Church in America, the Rev. Svend Marckman of the Bronx and the Rev. Dr. A. T. Dorf of Brooklyn. Other Americans of note where Elna was concerned were Mr. and Mrs. Emil Godiksen and Mr. and Mrs. A. C. Petersen, the dairymen of Hartford and Bloomfield. The Godiksens and the Petersens were participants in Niels Lund's folk dancing group in central Connecticut, the group of which Elna was also a member.

In the huge banquet hall Elna was assigned to table 74 together with a Hartford friend, Bertine Norregaard, who was also a member of Niels Lund's group. Elna did not know the other eight at her table, but it mattered little. Always interested in meeting new people - especially fellow Danes - Elna was at the Waldorf Astoria that night to focus on the royal guests. Throughout the evening Elna entertained flashbacks to her childhood when the King of Denmark visited her place of employment and lifted her high in an expression of love for her (she was eight years old) - a love he extended to all Danish citizens. And now it was to be a few hours with Crown Prince Frederik, her contemporary, and the son of the King who had hoisted her high thirty years before! What a thrill - to live in the present moment with a recollection of that earlier time in her life..

The program opened to a hushed audience with two Danish national songs sung by Povla Frijsh. A long list of speakers followed under the leadership of Toastmaster Thomas J. Watson, President of the International Chamber of Commerce. There was a brief address by the Honorable Fiorello H. La Guardia, Mayor of the City of New York, who welcomed all of the guests to New York. C. H. W. Hasselriis, Chairman of the American-Danish Committee to the New York World's Fair gloried in the moment and spoke eloquently of the event which was about to open on a reclaimed swamp. The Trilon and Perisphere, which served as centerpiece for the fair, became the hallmark of a future which the fair committee anticipated in the development of the International Exhibit. He also called attention to the building which was to serve as the Denmark building - a feature that he hoped the guests would have an opportunity to visit - perhaps even as early as June 5, 1939, the anniversary date of Denmark's decision to change its form of government from its historical unlimited monarchical form of government to a constitutional monarchy.

From time to time there was an opportunity to enjoy the music of the Copenhagen Orchestra with marches and music from Denmark - including pieces from "Elverhøj" by Kuhlau and the "Riberhus March" by Frøhlig.

Quietly the guests of the evening enjoyed a sumptuous feast of Tornados of Beef Rossini, with New Peas, Potatoes Lorette and Fresh California Asparagus with Vinagarette Sauce. The meal was topped off with Casanove Champagne 1928, Mousse of Kumquats with Strawberries, Chocolate Leaves and Macaroons. In a final tribute to things Danish the guests were served a demitasse of coffee and Peter F. Heering Cherry Brandy or Chocolate Liqueur.

Yes, the event recalled moments from Elna's young years as a domestic, but it also recalled for her the elegant years when she served as the housekeeper for Denmark's leading bachelor senator, who exposed her to the elegance which was in this moment being relived in the Waldorf Astoria event.

Music, memories, and more traveled with her to Hartford on that May 4, 1939, as she and Bertine Norrgaard reviewed the events of the evening before. The three-hour train trip on the New York, New Haven and Hartford Railroad vanished in the review, and soon the two ladies were at the Railroad Station on Asylum Avenue in Hartford. It was a short bus ride to 144 Putnam Street where Bertine stayed as a guest before the much longer bus ride to Farmington the next day. While

154

there was much more to talk about, the two dropped into bed exhausted from the round trip to New York.

It was not many days after their return from the gala event that both ladies were to be contacted for another day in New York. It was the day that C. H. W. Hasselriis had spoken about, viz. June 5, 1939 - *Grundlovsdag*. The Godiksens and the Petersens had remained in New York long enough to arrange for the participation of their folk dance group in the events of that important day at the fair. They were only to dance two squares, or numbers, but it was an event that could serve as an excellent sequel to the royal banquet on May 3rd in New York.

Emil Godiksen arranged for group transportation with the Connecticut Bus Company. Besides their regular activity of providing franchised transportation throughout central Connecticut the bus company also responded to request for charters. With the World's Fair only 110 miles from Hartford, the Connecticut Bus Company was well prepared to respond to the folk dancing Hartford Danes. The biggest obstacle lay before the members of the dancing group in arranging to be freed from their employment on assembly lines, delivery routes, and other activity which defined their work. One by one they reported their ability to participate in the planned activity.

The smaller group of six who had attended the royal banquet gathered up twelve more so that there now were eighteen from the greater Hartford area who could participate in a very unusual Danish-American event scheduled for June 5, 1939.

At meetings of Our Savior's Danish Lutheran Church and the Hartford Lodge of the Danish Brotherhood of America and at other meetings where Danish-Americans met, there was conversation about the joy of being Danes in America.

Grand View College

A New Day Dawns

The Year Nineteen-Thirty-Nine

Seventeen years had passed since Elna arrived in America when the year nineteen-thirty-nine appeared on the calendar. The twenty-two year old whose mission in nineteen-twenty-two was to deliver a younger sister to a childless aunt and uncle in the U.S.A. and return in "no time at all," now found herself with almost half of her life having been lived in America. Though she rarely defined it as such, Elna was living a dual citizenship with one foot in Denmark and one foot in America.

Dining with Danish royalty at the Waldorf Astoria in New York and participating in a presentation of Danish folk dancing at the World's Fair served to renew and strengthen Elna in her heritage. It was a milestone to record in her book of memories, where she could make note of her Danish strengths.

But nineteen-thirty-nine was a pivotal year which would bring her new strength for her American life. Immanent on the horizon was a major world war which was to sever (or hold in suspension) communication with her Danish roots. A ninety-day visit from her father, contrary to its intended purpose, served to sharpen well in advance the severance that was to be. The Laumark family in America was concerned about getting the "head of the household" back to Denmark before such a thing would become impossible. The apprehension of the Laumarks soon became a reality marked by their personal relief that their father had made it back to Denmark only weeks before the Nazi army marched on Poland.

With the invasion of Poland, and later the attack upon Pearl Harbor, traffic between the continents of Europe and North America came to a near standstill except for the military transports which were to make regular trips to Europe from America with troops whose task would be to gain victory over the madness of Adolph Hitler. All correspondence except occasional Red Cross letters ceased and that which fed many a European soul stopped. Reactions in America ranged from a deep sadness to a complete denial of roots in the European cultures. The spiritual depression that prevailed superseded any experience of economic depression which had been part of the American experience for many foreigners.

Fortunately for Elna, there was a change in the life of her church, Our Savior's Danish Lutheran Church. By late summer in 1938 Pastor Johannes Knudsen had begun his ministry to the "Danish Church" in

Hartford. With Pastor Knudsen's arrival in Hartford a dramatic change was about to take place. That change began with the amendment of the church's name to read "Our Savior's Lutheran Church." That very fact declared to all of the world, but most dramatically to the membership of the congregation, that Our Savior's Lutheran Church was to be an "American" church.

The first sign of that transformation was a rearrangement of the hours of worship so that the "holy" hour on Sunday would be "an Engliss Service." The Sunday morning schedule would now read: 8:30 a.m. - Danish Services; 9:30 a.m. - Sunday School; and 11:00 a.m. - English Services. Due to an emotional disfunction of the custodian of the church the sign concluded as it had for a half century or more: "*Alle Er Velkommen.*"

The little red songbooks - "*Børne Sangbogen*" - were stacked in the corner of a well-worn pew which backed up to the east wall of the church basement (*Undersalen*) together with other Sunday School material from the Danish Lutheran Publishing House of Blair, Nebraska, and the Danish Book Concern of Cedar Falls, Iowa. Other vestiges of the past included miniature Danish flags crowded into the corners of a variety of book cases which filled the classrooms.

Confirmation classes, which had been conducted in Danish - now were conducted in English and were reduced to a two-year cycle. There was still memory work, but that memory work consisted mostly of Bible verses together with a few choice Danish hymns, now translated, remaining as part of the instruction curriculum.

Most significant for the future of the congregation was a departure from the vacation school of six weeks in the summer - patterned after the Danish educational system - largely a local extension of the Church of Denmark. That school offered all of the courses taught in Denmark - mathematics, Danish history, Danish literature, gymnastics and conversational Danish. Taking the place of the six-week school was a week of living together at summer camp.

Considered an American expression of religious education for the new generation of Danish kids, the camp appealed to the young people of other District One congregations of the Danish Evangelical Lutheran Church in America. Young people of Sunday School age from Bridgeport and from the Ninth Street Church (Danish) in Brooklyn attended the camp - held at Sweetheart Lake in rural Stafford Springs, Connecticut.

Assembling at the church under Pastor Knudsen's leadership had now become fun as over against a sense of duty as it had been before

159

under the earlier pastoral leadership in the congregation. The new life which was to be found in Our Savior's Lutheran Church spawned a Thursday evening young peoples' meeting - open to all confirmed "young" people - the oldest of which was a lady of 92 years of age. She soon declared that she could no longer attend meetings regularly (a fact which had made itself known several years before her 92nd birthday) and that she should be dropped from the rolls!

The Young Peoples' meeting which had come into being with dramatic speed began to erode as one young man after another was drafted for service with the military forces of the United States. A project which kept the young ladies in attendance was preparing gift packages for the "boys in service." An honor roll with over thirty names of enlisted personnel was placed in a prominent place in the church basement for all to see. Bannered across the top of the honor roll was an American flag making it very clear that the focus of the worshipping group at the corner of Russ and Babcock Street was no longer Denmark but a whole world to which Danish Americans in that congregation looked with commitment for a world at peace.

Elna's children were a part of the pivotal changes which began in 1939. As they participated in the changes of the day - beginning with their own confirmation in 1939 - they shared with their mother, Elna Olsen, a new focus which immersed them in that which was truly American.

160

A New Decade of New Horizons

As Elna turned the calendar to January 1940, the decade of the 30s passed into review for her. Tremendous changes had taken place in her life - changes that immersed her in life in America. The decade of the twenties had brought her to America, but in that decade she had not been transplanted. The "planted" part of that idea had not yet really occurred. Most of her surroundings in those early years were Danish, albeit on American soil.

The decade of the 30s was very different. Those years were years of becoming "rooted in." Part of that "rooting in" began with Elna's employment at the Merrow Machine Company, an employment that exposed her to a variety of cultural expressions which over time had created the fabric to be labeled "America." Her children had become enrolled in the American schools. Her social life, what there was of it, was becoming more and more related to her neighborhood. What remained of her "Danish" life was rapidly fading into the past, except for that which related to her Christian Faith - a faith structured and expressed in the Danish culture and lived out in Our Savior's Danish Lutheran Church.

But now, the congregation of which she was a part had dropped the term "Danish" from its name and was becoming part of American religious life. That transition had been helped along with the leadership of Pastor Johannes V. Knudsen and stimulated by Pastor Knudsen's enrollment in the Hartford Theological Seminary from which he received a "doctor's degree" in the late spring of 1942. Whether by divine plan or hopeful anticipation by the Danish Evangelical Lutheran Church in America that degree prepared Pastor Knudsen for a call to serve as President of Grand View College and Dean of Grand View Theological Seminary, respectively.

Our Savior's Lutheran Church in Hartford had anticipated that something of that nature might occur - even as plans were being made to call Pastor (now Doctor) Knudsen to become the Pastor of Our Savior's Church, but it provided an answer for Our Savior's need for a pastor and, as it turned out to be an answer to the Danish Evangelical Lutheran Church's need for leadership of its most important institution.

Pastor Knudsen's ministry in Hartford and Doctor Knudsen's call to lead the college and seminary of the Danish Evangelical Lutheran Church in America had consequences beyond a pastoral vacancy for

Our Savior's Church. That move had a direct influence on the life of Elna that neither she nor anyone else could have anticipated. In performing his pastoral ministry, Pastor Knudsen had challenged all of the young men in his confirmation classes with the possibility of a career in the ministry. The first of those classes had included Elna's children in the last year of the 30s decade. Upon Pastor Knudsen's departure in 1942, the challenge was issued again and plans which had already secretly been in motion began to develop for Harold's enrollment in the fall of 1943 in the freshman class at Grand View College, the year that Harold graduated from Hartford Public High School.

For Harold that enrollment was to involve him in a seven-year program of preparation for the ministry. For Elna that enrollment was to involve her in a decade of travel to the Midwest to visit with her children, both of whom in that decade had enrolled at Grand View College, and back to Denmark twenty-five years later than had been planned when she accepted the assignment to deliver her 16 year old sister, Christine, to a childless aunt and uncle in South River, New Jersey. The later visits to the Midwest were for very important family occasions..

While there was only one visit to Europe, there were three visits to the Midwest. The first of those visits occurred when it became Alice's decision to follow her brother to Grand View College. With an empty nest for the first time in her life, Elna found it important to visit her children and to see for herself "what a wonderful place Grand View College is" - a report that she had received from both of her children from time to time.

Mrs. Marie Back, who had befriended Elna in the early years after her arrival in Hartford and who had taken a special interest in the two children, accompanied Elna in the spring of 1946. Marie, who managed to keep the young ladies in the women's dorm in stitches, had declared that she wanted to visit Pastor Valdemar Jensen in "Atlantic City," Iowa, thereby satisfying her two interests in Iowa in one trip. Visiting in the women's dorm became a near disaster on a number of occasions when Marie Back sat on the edge of the wing-tipped beds, designed to quickly accommodate two people when necessary, only to be dumped quickly to the floor. The sobering experiences came when the two ladies came to know as "real people" those who taught the young people - the faculty and staff: A.C. Nielsen, Peter Jorgensen, Arthur Ammentorp, Ernest D. Nielsen, Harald Knudsen, Helvina Mailand, Carl and Dagmar Eriksen and not least in importance, Pastor Johannes and Ellen

162

Knudsen, now old friends from Hartford. The entire experience recalled for Elna much of her own experience as a student at Roskilde Folk High School in Denmark and became a special joy to her.

A second trip was a weekend trip by train to attend the wedding of Harold to Lois A. Jensen of Des Moines in 1948. There was little time to drink of the cultural environment of the Midwest on that trip, but it was an event that could not be missed. It was an exhausting trip shored up only by the joy of the occasion.

The third trip came on the occasion of Harold's ordination into the ministry of the Danish Evangelical Lutheran Church in America in 1950. It was a festive occasion. "One of the best meetings of the Danish Church, ever," was the declaration of the Askov *American, a* weekly newspaper. The phrase fit Elna's emotions about the convention and especially the ordination service. There was a special joy in her heart as she shared in that event.

Never before had Elna seen so many clergy gathered in one place. Never before had she heard such powerful singing of hymnal favorites, albeit many of them in translation into English. Never before had liturgy and word penetrated so deeply into her soul. The nearly thirty years of life in America flashed through her soul. Dreams about the future darted quickly, but about one thing she was certain and that was that her faith would continue to find new and surprising expression in an America idiom. The future would bring her a faith couched in the American culture. Her head was filled with many things - memories and dreams - but her heart would glow as she silently returned to her Danish faith with the phrase expressed so often by her own mother, *"Gud, du ska' ha' tak!"*

Elna slept soundly the night of August twentieth, awakening early to the clock of the Eastern time zone, giving her plenty of time to be ready for the train that was to take her from Askov, Minnesota, to Minneapolis and from there to New York and Hartford. Once home, the church which had served her well became the territory in and through which she could serve - reaching out to the Maloneys, the Carambasis, the Tibedeaus, the Swenssons and others to whom the church could bring strength and comfort in the many changes of life. It would extend beyond her physical presence in the extension of her faith through her son of whom she had always been proud.

As she waved, "good bye," the phrase *"Gud, du ska' ha' tak!"* was clearly in her heart and on her lips. Tearfully she waved as the train slowly pulled away from the station.

Post Script

Elna lived many years beyond the events of this book. She died in her sleep at the Washington National Lutheran Home in Rockville, Maryland, where she had lived for twelve years, on May 26, 1999 - four and a half months short of one-hundred years. The Rev. Dr. Richard Reichardt, Administrator of the Home, presided at her funeral.

Index

Other Books by Lur Publications

Tante Johanne
Letters of a Danish Immigrant Family
1887-1910
Letters and photographs
with commentary by John W. Nielsen
118 pp. ISBN 0-930697-01-4
$12.95 plus shipping

Many Danes, Some Norwegians
Karen Miller's Diary - 1894
With photographs and commentary
by John W. Nielsen
173 pp. ISBN 0-930697-02-2
$14.95 plus shipping

A Frame but no Picture
The story of a boy left behind
in Denmark
Edited by John W. Nielsen
63 pp. ISBN 0-930697-03-0
$8.50 plus shipping

Embracing Two Worlds:
The Thorvald Muller Family
of Kimballton
Edited by:
Barbara Lund-Jones & John W. Nielsen
180 pp. ISBN 0-930697-04-9
$14.95 plus shipping

Passages from India:
Letters, Essays, and Poems
1944-1946
by Norman C. Bansen
201 pp. ISBN 0-930697-05-7
$19.95 plus shipping

Boats in the Night
Knud Dyby's Story
of Resistance and Rescue
by Martha Loeffler
140 pp. ISBN 0-930697-07-3
$14.95 plus shipping

Our Last Frontiers:
A World Cruise Diary
by Borge and Lotte Christensen
238 pp. ISBN 0-930697-08-1
$22.50 plus shipping

Under the Clouds
by Dagmar E. Vasby
and Charlene M. Luchterhand
142 pp. ISBN 0-930697-09-X
$14.95 plus Shipping

Danes in America:
Danish-American Lutheranism
from 1860 to 1908
by Peder Kolhede, Peter Sorensen Vig,
Ivar Marius Hansen
200 pp. ISBN 0-930697-10-3
$22.50 plus shipping

Inside the Fighting First:
Papers of a Nebraska Private in the
Philippine War
by Thomas Solevad Nielsen & Matthew
Plowman
188 pp. ISBN 0-930697-11-1
$19.95 plus shipping

Danes in America:
Kansas and Nebraska
Translated by Nina Engskow
Edited by John W. Nielsen
126 pp. ISBN 0-930697-12-x
$16.50 plus shipping

Attracted to America
Edited by Ivan E. Nielsen
164 pp. ISBN 0-930697-13-8
$19.95 plus shipping

Peter S. Petersen Memoirs
Edited by John W. Nielsen
248 pp. ISBN 0-930697-14-6
$27.50 plus shipping

Order from: Lur Publications
Danish Immigrant Archive
Dana College
Blair, Nebraska 68008

Lur Publications takes its name from the graceful bronze age horns found in Scandinavian museums. Just as today when those horns are blown, sounds from an ancient past are heard, so these books give voice to a less distant Danish past.

Lur Publications Policies

Lur Publications is committed to the publication of materials that relate to the Danish American experience. To achieve this goal it encourages research and scholarship on Danish immigrant subjects, on the life and contributions of their descendants, and on connections between Denmark and Danes abroad. Significant in achieving this goal is making available to the general public materials in the Danish Immigrant Archive - Dana College. In its basic purpose Lur Publications complements the goals of the Danish American Heritage Society.

A further aim is to promote the collection, preservation, cataloging and use of written materials produced and received by Danish immigrants and their descendants. Such materials are welcomed by the respective Danish Immigrant Archives located at Dana College and Grand View College. Artifacts associated with Danish immigrants are sought by the Danish Immigrant Museum in Elk Horn, Iowa.

Scholars wishing to submit manuscripts for consideration are invited to contact Lur Publications, Danish Immigrant Archive, Dana College, Blair, Nebraska 68008-1041, (402) 426-7910, FAX: (402) 426-7332, e-mail: jwnielse@acad2.dana.edu

 ## Lur Publications Personnel

General Editor: Dr. John W. Nielsen
Advisory Board: Dr. Myrvin Christopherson, Dr. Brian Viets, Dr. John Mark Nielsen, Thomas S. Nielsen, Ruth Rasmussen